V&R unipress

SPECLANG
Beiträge zur Berufs- und Fachkommunikation

Band 3

Herausgegeben von
Beata Grzeszczakowska-Pawlikowska, Jacek Makowski
und Agnieszka Stawikowska-Marcinkowska

Die Bände dieser Reihe sind peer-reviewed.

Karolina Puchała-Ladzińska

Interpreting: an Art, a Craft or a Superpower?

With 20 figures

V&R unipress

Bibliografische Information der Deutschen Nationalbibliothek
Die Deutsche Nationalbibliothek verzeichnet diese Publikation in der Deutschen
Nationalbibliografie; detaillierte bibliografische Daten sind im Internet über
https://dnb.de abrufbar.

© 2024 Brill | V&R unipress, Robert-Bosch-Breite 10, D-37079 Göttingen, ein Imprint der Brill-Gruppe
(Koninklijke Brill NV, Leiden, Niederlande; Brill USA Inc., Boston MA, USA; Brill Asia Pte Ltd,
Singapore; Brill Deutschland GmbH, Paderborn, Deutschland; Brill Österreich GmbH, Wien,
Österreich)
Koninklijke Brill NV umfasst die Imprints Brill, Brill Nijhoff, Brill Schöningh, Brill Fink, Brill mentis,
Brill Wageningen Academic, Vandenhoeck & Ruprecht, Böhlau und V&R unipress.

Umschlagabbildung: Gehirn Geist Psychologie, ElisaRiva (https://pixabay.com/de/illustrations/
gehirn-geist-psychologie-idee-2062057/)
Druck und Bindung: CPI books GmbH, Birkstraße 10, D-25917 Leck
Printed in the EU.

Vandenhoeck & Ruprecht Verlage | www.vandenhoeck-ruprecht-verlage.com

ISSN 2750-6169
ISBN 978-3-8471-1682-0

Contents

Introduction

Practical classes in interpreting are typically included in the curricula at universities offering translation specialization within the course in philology or applied linguistics at the BA and MA levels. Nowadays, when some classes are still conducted online, teachers responsible for interpreting-related subjects face a challenging task: on the one hand, they need to conduct classes in an attractive way that would be appealing to the new generation of students brought up in the era of ubiquitous technology, on the other hand, however, they must also provide them with the opportunity to develop their interpreting competences and skills that are sought after in the job market.

Therefore, the purpose of this publication is not only to present (in a, hopefully, approachable form) certain theoretical issues related to interpreting (such as the history and types of interpreting, the competence of interpreters, the role of creativity in interpreting, to name but a few), but also to provide some practical ideas and ready-made exercises and activities to be used with students of interpreting, whether in a traditional or a virtual classroom. The exercises compiled at the end of this book are related to, for instance, taking notes in consecutive interpreting, developing memory, attention divisibility and creative thinking, making decisions and solving interpreting problems, developing flexible thinking – i. e. the skills that every successful interpreter needs in order to perform well.

I hope that the book will fill the gap on the publishing market in Poland, where there is a shortage of publications that would address the problem of interpreting, especially from the practical perspective, offering some ready-made exercises to be used when working with students. The majority of publications concerning interpreting were published before the year 2020, when the coronavirus pandemic radically changed the face of education around the world and forced educators to quickly come up with and apply new methods and forms of teaching.

The first chapter of the book presents some basic theoretical issues related to interpreting – definitions, history and the most popular types of interpreting, such as consecutive, simultaneous, *a vista* and community interpreting, together with their specific nature. The second chapter discusses the competences and skills of an interpreter, which have been divided into knowledge and linguistic skills, as well as non-linguistic ones such as memory, attention, focus, anticipation and stress management. Chapter three focuses on note-taking as an aid for consecutive interpreting and discusses the role of notes, explains how to take notes, and how to use symbols and abbreviations. In chapter four, interpreting is presented as a process in which the proper selection of techniques and strategies is of paramount importance. This part of the publication also addresses the problem of errors in interpreting, non-verbal elements, as well as interpreting assessment. The fifth chapter focuses on the role of creative thinking in the context of interpreting – it defines the concept of creativity, presents interpreting as a creative process, which consists of creative products, creative thought processes (such as decision making and problem solving) and creative behaviours of the interpreter. The sixth chapter discusses the interpreter training in Poland, presents and characterizes interpreting norms, as well as describes professional associations of interpreters. The last chapter offers a selection of practical exercises and activities for interpreting trainees, which have been divided into those related to consecutive interpreting (memory, note-taking, information processing, production), and those that can be used to practice simultaneous interpreting (para-interpreting exercises, information processing and production in simultaneous interpreting).

The primary target readers for this book are students of translation and interpreting specializations within the course of English Philology and Applied Linguistics, teachers conducting interpreting classes at universities and other institutes of higher education, as well as all those who are interested in interpreting and wish to broaden their knowledge and develop their skills and competences in this field.

I believe that the publication will also be useful in developing the translation and interpreting specialization at the Department of English Studies of the University of Rzeszów, and will prove helpful not only for students preparing for the future profession of interpreters, but also for instructors teaching interpreting, since, in addition to discussing some theoretical issues, the book constitutes a practical guide to designing and conducting interpreting classes, regardless of whether they take place face-to-face or online. It is also my sincere hope that the book will find its readership among academic teachers employed at other Polish universities and institutes of higher education and teaching interpreting both traditionally and via online platforms.

Chapter 1:
What is Interpreting?

1.1 Definition

Interpreting (Polish: *przekład ustny*) is a type of natural interlinguistic mediation which appeared together with the development of languages and pre-dates the creation of alphabets (Tryuk 2007, 15). In many Indo-European languages the term "interpreting" has its own history reaching as far back as to the times of Assyria and Babylon (Pöchhacker 2016).

Also etymology of the term "translator" is quite complex. In the translation of the Bible from Aramaic one may find the term *meturgeman* (meaning "translator"), which comes from the Assyrian *ragam* meaning "to speak", which, in turn, derives from *rigamu* ("word") and *taf'el* (i.e. "one that helps in communication") (Tryuk 2007, 15). *Meturgeman* and the related term – *turgeman* – were then adopted by other Middle Eastern languages such as Turkish and Arabic, but also by some European languages like French (where they evolved into *truchement*) and English (*dragoman*). These terms are still used today to mean "guide" or "translator" (ibidem).

The Italian term *interprete* comes from the Latin *interpress*. "Interpreting", in Italian *interpretazione* (deriving from the Latin *inter* meaning "between" and *pretium* meaning "price"), was intended to help two or several persons to reach an agreement, typically to agree on a price in barter trade (Merlini 2005, 20). This emphasis on negotiation and parties agreement in language interpretation has been preserved today (Dublanc 2008, 149).

Terminologia tłumaczenia, translated and adapted by Tomaszkiewicz (2004), states that interpreting (Polish: *tłumaczenie ustne*) is a translator's activity which, simultaneously or consecutively, allows two or more interlocutors, who do not speak the same language, to communicate by means of words or gestures (2004, 108). Services of professional interpreters are used, for instance, in courts, during international meetings and conferences, diplomatic missions, parliamentary or other political meetings (ibidem).

With a view to better understand the discipline itself, as well as shed some light on its roots, the following section is going to have a closer look at the history of interpreting.

1.2   History

Although the profession of the translator itself was recognized only in the 20th century, the role and the function of a translator have very old roots (Van Hoof 1962, 9, after Dublanc 2008, 150). It is an undeniable fact that the spoken word is much older than the written one. As observed by Dublanc (ibidem), since the fall of the Tower of Babel, which symbolized the split in linguistic unity, translation became necessary to facilitate communication between people. It was the primary medium of exchange between ethnic groups speaking different languages and cultivating different traditions.

The oldest traces of translations can be found in the Egyptian civilization, with the first records dating back to around 3000 BC. Several centuries later, Egypt had some translators in its army – some of them participated in war expeditions against the barbarians, whereas others were sent with the sailors to conquer the East (Van Hoof 1962, 9–11, after Dublanc 2008, 150).

It was during this period that disciplines such as diplomacy started developing, in which translators would play an instrumental role, at least in the Roman Empire. The ancient Greeks, however, did not attach great importance to translation, nor did they recognize the need to learn foreign languages (ibidem). Dublanc (2008, 150) refers to this phenomenon as a sort of "cultural snobbism", meaning that the Greeks believed in their own cultural superiority, claiming that it was foreigners who should learn Greek in order to be able to communicate with them. This attitude towards other communities suggests that the work of a translator was not valued highly in the Greek civilization, and it was only in the Roman times that it received proper recognition.

In ancient Rome one could find numerous traces of translatory activities. Learning foreign languages enjoyed prestige and in certain parts of the Empire some citizens were bilingual, fluent in two languages. Since both Latin and Greek were taught in schools, anyone had the opportunity to learn these languages at a young age (Tryuk 2007, 17). Translators in ancient Rome were employed in the administration to facilitate contact with the conquered nations. They often took part in war expeditions. A translator who participated in military campaigns enjoyed great respect and was called *vir sanctus* (literally: "a holy man") (Tryuk 2007, 18). Translators were also of great assistance during meetings with senators or Greek philosophers, helping to make the conversation more efficient (Dublanc 2008, 151).

However, as regards interpreting, Woodsworth and Delisle (2012, 248) observe that research into its history is relatively new. For a long time the main scholarly interest concerned professional conference interpreting, and the history of interpreting received little academic attention. Until the 1990s, only a limited number of publications were available on the subject (Pöchhacker 2016, 152). Furthermore, history books generally failed to include interpreters and their work (Woodsworth and Delisle 2012, 247). This might have stemmed from the dominance of the written text over the spoken word, as well as the fact that those who were producing written texts were more likely to be recorded by historians (ibidem). A similar opinion is expressed by Baigorri-Jalón (2006, 102) who says that

> "[t]ranslation and interpreting differ in one important aspect: translation deals with written texts and interpreting with oral speeches (complemented by non-verbal information). Historical research is usually associated with documents, to the extent that we define prehistory as the period from which documents – in a large sense – are not available".

This entails that those attempting to delve into the history of interpreting are faced with a considerable problem, i. e. that of the sources (ibidem). Besides, as observed by Pöchhacker (2016, 152), interpreting was long perceived as a supportive activity, not worthy of any particular attention, and interpreters did not generally enjoy a high social status.

Despite the shortage of information sources regarding this particular area of study, interpreting is believed to exist since the ancient times. The profession of an interpreter was first mentioned in the third millennium AC and could be found in numerous inscriptions on the Elephantine Princes' funeral monuments. As for this particular period of time, there are also hieroglyphics which prove that services of interpreters were used in Egypt and in the Persian Empire.[1]

In the era of the Middle Ages, interpreting was taught in translation schools such as the School of Translators in Toledo, where not only the written translations but also their oral versions were often produced. In the period of the Crusades, interpreters, also referred to at that time as "dragomen," became so important and their assistance so indispensable that some scholars consider this era as the birth of modern diplomatic interpreting.[2]

During the Modern Age, interpreters, particularly the Spanish ones, played an instrumental role in the great discoveries of the 15th and 16th centuries. The rules for interpreters living on the American continent, which were established at that time, were also valid during the 16th and 17th centuries.[3]

---

1 http://linkterpreting.uvigo.es/historia/?lang=en, accessed 4. 02. 2023.
2 Ibidem.
3 Ibidem.

In the 19th century, interpreting began to play an increasingly more significant role in the diplomatic and political fields, resulting in professional interpreters receiving more recognition and their names becoming more and more well-known. Also around this time, certain rules were established to regulate the profession of court interpreters.[4]

The interpreting profession experienced a significant breakthrough only at the beginning of the 20th century due to the appearance of a new specialization within the profession: the conference interpreter. This suddenly became a very sought-out function since, at that time, any person who could serve as a communication link between military units speaking different languages, was particularly valuable to the war machine. Such professionals were called war interpreters.

While discussing conference interpreting, Baigorri-Jalón (2006, 101–102) mentions Joseph Belleau, a lawyer from Quebec, who, in 1919, was hired as an interpreter to take part in the international conference (the Paris Peace Conference), and considers him to be a pioneer in conference interpreting. At this conference, the representatives of four of the victorious countries (United States, United Kingdom, France and Italy) met to discuss a series of topics that would eventually lead to the signing of the Treaty of Versailles and the formation of the League of Nations. The Paris Peace Conference is considered to be the first major multilateral conference in which interpreting was systematically used in the two official languages: English and French. This means that the conference speakers were using one of these two languages and an interpreter was rendering the speech into the other official language.[5] The said conference was held in Washington and thanks to it, the International Labor Organization (ILO) was initiated. Baigorri-Jalón (2006, 102) points out that "the ILO was an institution in the 1920s in which interpreting constituted an element of democratization, since up until then workers did not have linguistic means of communication that allowed them to feel comfortable in international gatherings".

In the interwar period the League of Nations (LN) was formed with its official languages being English and French. What this entailed was that if speakers wanted to deliver their speeches in any language other than these two, they had to provide their own interpreters. As regards interpreting modes, the LN – having only two official languages – predominantly used the consecutive one, which proved effective in an organization having such a limited number of languages. However, the consecutive mode was much less efficient in the ILO which was using a larger number of languages. Therefore, the need for the simultaneous interpreting arose (Tryuk 2007, 24–25). However, the LN was rather reluctant to

4 Ibidem.
5 Ibidem.

adopt this interpreting method – the interpreters themselves were unwilling to use this mode, considering it a threat to their status and position. As a result, simultaneous interpreting did not become popular until more than ten years later, during the Nuremberg Trials, which were held in Germany after the end of World War II. The participants were Great Britain, United States, France and the Soviet Union. Due to this linguistic diversity, consecutive interpreting turned out to be ineffective as it was deemed too time-consuming (Tryuk 2007, 33) and, finally, simultaneous interpreting ended up as the chosen method. However, the earlier predominance of consecutive interpreting entailed that there were very few well-trained simultaneous interpreters. The selected candidates were frequently only offered a short and brief training in which they practiced with simulated trials. Some of them were not even provided with this basic training (Tryuk 2007, 35). Additionally, they had to cope with technical and logistics difficulties, as well as the spoken speed of the speakers.[6]

Since the end of the World War II, the interpreting profession has developed significantly. One of the essential changes is the continuous development of simultaneous interpreting which surpassed the consecutive mode and offered numerous benefits during international meetings, such as a more authentic and lively rendition of speeches and conversations, as well as time- and cost-effectiveness (Tryuk 2007, 39). Progress in the field of interpreting is also evidenced by its consolidation as a profession, the emergence of more specialized training courses, as well as the implementation of stricter selection processes for candidates aspiring to interpret for international organizations.[7]

Despite all that is known about the history of interpreting, given the limited sources on the subject, one may definitely say that interpreting, as an activity, probably goes as far back as to the prehistoric times, where different human groups came into contact with each other. Nevertheless, as a profession, and in the understanding of academics, practitioners, and society in general, interpreting has become recognized and defined only recently (ibidem). Why is it so important to find out about and study the history of interpreting? Baigorri-Jalón (2006, 103) provides an answer to this question stating that "the vision of the first attempts at simultaneous interpreting by consecutive interpreters was not the same as that of subsequent generations", and adding that:

"[…] understanding of history can help professionals, trainers and trainees face the natural changes experienced in all disciplines with technological evolution and can help researchers predict how new trends will evolve. For example, the reactions of current professionals to information technologies and remote interpreting can be understood

---

6 Ibidem.
7 Ibidem.

in the framework of similar reactions in the past to simultaneous interpreting devices" (ibidem).

The scholar also points out that interpreters should perceive the history of their profession as having a predictive value for future generations of interpreters who, knowing the history, will be able to take advantage of it and learn some lessons from past experience. Certainly, this is a field of study which still requires further in-depth research. The results of this research may also prove relevant and useful for many professionals and scholars engaged in other fields of study and research.

After this brief overview of the history of interpreting in general, let us now have a closer look at the most common interpreting types: consecutive, simultaneous, *a vista* and community interpreting.

1.3 Types of Interpreting

1.3.1 Consecutive Interpreting

Consecutive interpreting is a mode of interpreting, whereby the interpreter takes notes during the speech, and then recreates the speaker's message, uttering it to the audience, with the assistance of notes taken when listening to the speech. Usually, he or she stands or sits close to the speaker, listens and at the same time takes notes on a piece of paper, and afterwards translates the contents of the original speech through the microphone as soon as the speaker has finished delivering a certain fragment.[8]

As stated on the official website of the European Commission,[9] in order to become a good consecutive interpreter, one needs to have highly developed active listening skills, the ability to analyze the speaker's utterances, to take notes that will help them remember the speaker's message, and finally, to recreate the contents of the source language speech in a manner that sounds like a natural speech delivered in the target language. Therefore, the three main stages of consecutive interpreting are as follows:
1) active listening (understanding the original message);
2) analysis (structured notes taken when listening to the original speech);
3) reconstruction (communicating the original message in the target language with the assistance of notes).[10]

---

8 https://ec.europa.eu/education/knowledge-centre-interpretation/conference-interpreting/consecutive-interpreting_pl, accessed 11.07.2022.
9 Ibidem.
10 Ibidem.

Every single one of these stages differs significantly from the nature of similar stages in other professions. For instance, active listening entails listening not in order to react or join the conversation, but to remember and then both faithfully and accurately reproduce in the target language what has just been conveyed in the source language. In order to acquire this particular skill, interpreters typically first learn how to recreate the message without taking notes.

The second stage mentioned, namely analysis, requires one to develop the skill of prioritizing information, distinguishing between primary and secondary information, as well as correctly noting who said what, when something happened, and what the speaker's opinion about it is, etc. (the key questions the interpreter needs to answer when delivering the translation are: who?, what?, when?, where?, how?).

The third and final stage of consecutive interpreting, i.e. recreating what has been heard, requires other competences such as access to short-term memory, understanding the notes and the ability to deliver the original message in a way that would be interesting to the audience.

Saehu (2018) also distinguished three stages of consecutive interpreting, naming and explaining them as follows (Saehu 2018, 57–61; Maulida and Saehu 2022, 132–137):

1. Pre Interpreting – which means briefing with the organizer, and/or the speaker, the preparation concerning the topic to be discussed and that would be interpreted, as well as signing the contract. "The standard practice among conference interpreters is to obtain background materials from the conference organizer prior to the meeting and study them to gain a basic understanding of the subject and the specialized vocabulary" (Maulida and Saehu 2022, 136).

2. Whilst Interpreting – which is the main stage, involving the interpreter making eye contact with the audience, analyzing the discourse using his/her background knowledge, and maintaining the stability of sound production. This stage also involves note-taking with the use of symbols, abbreviations, and other forms of written language that are easily understood by the interpreter. Effective note-taking entails reducing words to ideas and transforming the ideas into symbols that can then be expressed in another language. Therefore, attempting to write down everything the speaker says word for word would be futile since a number of words may indicate just a single idea. Hence, it would be pointless to try to jot down every word uttered by the speaker, but the interpreter should rather note down the main ideas in various forms (words, symbols, pictures, etc.) that will later on help them recall the message and include the crucial information. In fact, there are numerous sources of such symbols, abbreviations or pictures, available to the interpreter. It does not matter what symbols are used as long as they are applied

consistently, quickly, and serve as a sort of "prompters", allowing the interpreter to easily retrieve the original message and all the relevant information included in the source language speech.[11]

3. Post Interpreting – which entails the interpreter maintains professionalism and confidentiality, as well as refrains from attempting to profit from any information disclosed during their work. It may also involve self-reflection and reviewing the effectiveness of the interpreting after having performed it.

The interpreter rendering a speech in the consecutive mode needs to perform a series of cognitive activities (entailed by the previously mentioned stages), i.e. attending to the message, focusing on the task at hand, recalling the message, understanding its meaning, visioning the message nonverbally and, finally, constructing the message in the target language (Ferryanti 2017, 3). During the entire process the interpreter typically sits or stands beside the speaker, listens and takes notes while the speaker is delivering the speech, and, when the speaker pauses or stops speaking, the interpreter delivers the message already in the target language (ibidem). This entails that the interpreter only has a few seconds to select the equivalents for the source language utterances before transferring the message to the listener(s) (Maulida and Saehu 2022, 128).

Maulida and Saehu (2022, 127) observe that in certain circumstances, consecutive interpreting brings with itself considerable advantages as it allows the interpreter to provide a more exact and comprehensive message.

Another popular interpreting mode is the simultaneous one which is going to be discussed in the following section.

1.3.2 Simultaneous Interpreting

According to the information provided on the website of the European Commission, simultaneous interpreting is "a mode of interpreting in which the speaker makes a speech and the interpreter reformulates the speech into a language his audience understands at the same time (or simultaneously). Simultaneous interpreters work in an interpreting booth (though they may also be using a *bidule* (portable interpretation equipment without a booth) or whispering (chuchotage)".[12]

---

11 More information on the role and principles governing note-taking in consecutive interpreting, as well as the symbols and abbreviations used, can be found in Chapter 3.

12 https://ec.europa.eu/education/knowledge-centre-interpretation/en/conference-interpreting/simultaneous-interpreting, accessed 7.02.2023.

Consistent with this definition is the one provided by Gile (2018, 531) who states that simultaneous interpreting is the one "in which the interpreter produces his/her speech while the interpreted speaker is speaking/signing – though with a lag of up to a few seconds". He also observes that simultaneous interpreting may or may not involve electronic equipment (such as microphones, headsets, interpreting booths), and is typically conducted in teams of at least two interpreters. They take turns interpreting every thirty minutes or so, since the pressure and the required level of concentration are so high that the task would be exhausting to perform by just one person (Gile 2018, 532).

The skills required from the simultaneous interpreter are similar to those that apply to consecutive interpreters as well, since the three main actions to be performed by the interpreter are essentially the same, whether it is a consecutive or a simultaneous mode. These are: active listening (combined with the understanding of the source language message), analysis (of the source language message as well as its structure), reproduction (i. e. communicating the source language message in the target language).[13]

As the European Commission website states, the essential difference between consecutive and simultaneous interpreting as regards the above stages is that in the latter all of them need to occur at the same time. This entails that apart from the skills required from a consecutive interpreter, like the already mentioned active listening, ability to prioritize information and distinguish between primary and secondary information, activating short-term memory, communication skills, etc., a professional simultaneous interpreter also needs to be capable of predicting what the speaker is going to say. This proves to be of particular importance when the speaker's language (i. e. the source language) differs considerably in terms of its syntactical structure from the language it is being interpreted into (i. e. the target language). Good stress management, as well as the ability to work well under pressure are indispensable in this profession.[14]

The simultaneous mode entails that the interpreter is under more pressure since the action of speaking needs to happen at the same time as listening and analyzing. Hence the need, and an even greater one than in the consecutive mode, for perfect mother-tongue skills, as well as excellent command of the second language. Also, in the simultaneous interpreting there is a much greater risk of language "interference", i. e. "an act of transferring patterns and elements of one linguistic system into another"[15] (Łuczyński and Maćkiewicz 2002, 111). In the interpreting practice this entails the interpreter's tendency to copy and claque

---

13 Ibidem.
14 Ibidem.
15 "[Interferencja, inaczej mówiąc, polega na] przenoszeniu wzorów i elementów jakiegoś systemu językowego do systemu innego". Author's own translation.

words, expressions and grammatical structures from the source language to the target language. Interference may concern virtually all language dimensions: phonological, morphological, syntactic, lexical, stylistic, etc. (Tomaszkiewicz 2006, 44). Therefore, simultaneous interpreters need to pay even more attention to their output, for instance by not copying the original syntax, dividing long sentences into shorter ones, as well as avoiding "false friends."[16]

All the above-mentioned complexities involved in simultaneous interpreting help to explain why novice interpreters need to learn consecutive interpreting first, and only then do they progress to the simultaneous mode. As already mentioned, although both modes require the same skills, the simultaneous one involves additional layers of complexity and difficulty, which have to practised and learnt step by step.

As stated by Giles (2018, 532), the predominant advantage of simultaneous interpreting over the consecutive mode is that the former saves time, especially when more than two languages are used. However, its main drawback is its higher cost. This stems from both the cost of the interpreting booth and electronic equipment, as well as the fact that simultaneous interpreters work in teams of at least two people, while consecutive interpreters often work alone. Another significant drawback of the simultaneous mode, as mentioned by Giles (ibidem) is lack of flexibility due to the use of booths and electronic equipment, with restricts mobility and requires a specific layout of the conference room.

A mode of interpreting which has certain common features with the simultaneous one is *a vista* interpreting, also referred to as sight translation. The following subchapter is going to have a closer look at this particular mode.

1.3.3 *A Vista* Interpreting (Sight Translation)

A vista interpreting, also known as sight translation (ST), is one of the basic modes of interpreting. As all other types of translation and interpreting, the process of sight translation also involves language transfer from the source language into the target language, but, contrary to other modes, it entails the change from a written form into an oral one. Here, the interpreter does not work in a booth and does not typically hear the original, but rather he/she is provided with the text in the source language and is expected to instantly and smoothly deliver its contents in the target language at a speed appropriate for natural oral production (Čeňková 2010, 320). Due to the inclusion of both the written and the

---

16 A false friend is "a word that is often confused with a word in another language with a different meaning because the two words look or sound similar" (https://dictionary.camb ridge.org/dictionary/english/false-friend, accessed 7.02.2023).

oral form of information processing, some scholars, such as Lambert (2004, 298), treat sight translation as both a special type of written translation, and a variant of interpreting. Hence, as observed by Żmudzki (2012, 731), sight translation entails a double transformation: from the source language into the target language and from the written to the oral form, thus it is an example of translational transmediality. Therefore, it seems logical to treat sight translation as a kind of hybrid between oral and written translation and, as Nader-Cioszek (2016, 39) observes, some scholars tend to perceive it so.

In sight translation the interpreter begins the entire process with the reception of the source text and, while reading it, he/she performs its conceptual reconstruction by identifying individual concepts, forming hypotheses for further development of textual macroconceptualization, identifying intertextual, intersemiotic and cultural references in the source text, analyzing it in terms of its communicative function, thematic scope, degree of "specialization", belonging to a specific type (Nader-Cioszek 2016, 39). Żmudzki (2013, 183) states that this entire analysis of the source text is also done with a view to assess the knowledge of the target recipients, their cognitive skills, as well as to determine their receptive skills for processing texts involving specialized terminology. The reception of the source text is followed by the transfer and production of the translation, consistent with the target language and culture. An additional difficulty involved in sight translation is the fact that cognitive conceptualization of the target text happens almost simultaneously with the translation process.

Characteristic features of sight translation are (Agrifoglio 2004; Gile 2005; Dragsted and Gorm Hansen 2009; Pöchhacker 2004, Sandrelli 2003, after Obidina 2015, 92):

1. Reception conditions:
   - written source-text presentation;
   - absence of author;
   - presence of punctuation;
   - permanent access to the text;
   - attention-sharing between visual input and oral output;
   - non-sequential reception (the reader can return to some fragments);
   - interpreter-paced (not paced by the speaker).
2. Production conditions:
   - oral target-text presentation;
   - time delay between the source language production and translation;
   - monitoring production while reading;
   - prior access to information (preliminary reading) / progressive access to new information (first sight translation);
   - considerable risk of interference;
   - interpreter-paced (not paced by the speaker);

- time-saving (in comparison to written translation);
- no assistance of colleagues.

Sight translation might be applied in a wide range of situations, including meetings, during which written documentation (e.g. annual and financial reports) is provided in the source language, whether in full or in selected fragments. It is also frequently used at press conferences where statements or press releases are delivered by an interpreter in a language which the audience understands (Čeňková 2010, 320).

As Čeňková (ibidem) observes, sight translation saves time during presentations and ceremonies as only the first paragraph that the speaker wrote down in his/her mother tongue is interpreted consecutively, whereas the rest is sight translated by the interpreter. This interpretation mode may also be applied at international conferences when someone wants to speak in another language (outside of the conference working languages) and when simultaneous interpreting for this particular language is not provided. Sight translation may also be employed to brief a client before an important event, particularly if the client does not have enough time get familiarized with the documents in the source language (ibidem).

The advantage of sight translation, from the interpreter's perspective, is that it allows them to set their own pace and does not require them to follow the speaker as is the case in the simultaneous mode. However, sight translation increases the risk of language interference and the tendency to calque the source language structure because the source text is constantly in front of the interpreter. The interpreter also faces the need to maintain eye contact with the audience, as well as needs to avoid unnecessary corrections or reformulations while translating. The idea is that the translation and delivery should be as natural as possible, while observing the target language norms, grammar, lexicon, sentence structure and syntax (Čeňková 2010, 321).

The benefits of sight translation, from the perspective of a trainee interpreter, include: a good practice in quick reading, improving text orientation, non-linear approach to text and identification of the main information, practice in avoiding linguistic interferences and in breaking free from the original form, a useful tool in preparation for simultaneous interpreting (Jiménez Ivars 2008, after Čeňková 2010, 322). By practising sight translation, both interpreting novices as well as professional interpreters, learn to

"[...] anticipate, generalise and filter out less important details under time and linguistic pressure; activate vocabulary and quick response in the target language; break up long and complex sentences; fluently communicate with the audience; and transmit the message without repetitions and unnecessary corrections" (Čeňková 2010, 322).

Having briefly discussed the three most popular interpreting modes – consecutive, simultaneous and *a vista* interpreting – it is now time to move on to the final interpreting type to be described here, namely community interpreting, the details of which will be provided in the following subchapter.

1.3.4 Community Interpreting

Community interpreting is a type of service used in community-based situations. It is particularly employed in communities with large numbers of ethnic minorities, and it allows them to have access to various services they would not be able to access otherwise due to the language barrier (Pöchhacker 1999, 26). This definition is consistent with another one, provided by Hertog (2010),[17] who states that "[c]ommunity interpreting (CI) takes place to enable individuals or groups in society who do not speak the official or dominant language of the services provided by central or local government to access these services and to communicate with the service providers". Community interpreting may involve not only spoken language interpreting but also sign-language interpreting (Pöchhacker 1999, 26).

This type of interpreting takes place in a wide variety of contexts, and some of its typical settings are social services such as welfare, housing, employment or schools; medical settings like child care centres, hospitals and clinics; or legal settings such as prisons, police stations or probation offices (ibidem). This plethora of contexts and settings entails that the community interpreter needs to be able to quickly and flexibly switch between different interpreting modes, as well as select the appropriate interpreting strategy. For instance, he/she may choose to perform consecutive interpreting with note-taking to render an immigrant's narrative or to interpret a witness's speech in court, but apply simultaneous interpreting (in the form of chuchotage) for a single client during the closing arguments of the prosecution in court or during parents' school meetings. Community interpreters are also frequently expected to perform sight translation of various personal and official documents, as well as do telephone or videoconferencing interpreting (ibidem).

Community interpreters are required to have a fluent command of the language they are interpreting, as well as be familiar with the public services involved, being aware of the cultural implications of their interpreting work. They are also required to abide by the Interpreter's Code of Ethics (Pöchhacker 1999, 26).

---

17 https://benjamins.com/online/hts/articles/comm3, accessed 12.02.2023.

As observed by Bowen (2022),[18] the clients of community interpreters are typically immigrants, refugees of all age groups, migrant workers and their children. Even if they have been living in their host country for many years, their local community where they have been surrounded mainly by their compatriots (for instance New York's "Little Italy" or the Polish area of Chicago), has largely eliminated the necessity to learn English until they need to access some public services such as social security or health care.

Since the clients may come from various countries and backgrounds, the range of languages needed for community interpreting is considerable. Also the language level required may be quite different from that in other types of interpreting due to regional variations and dialects which may pose difficulties. An additional challenge might be caused by the client's individual situation and their mental condition, as well as emotions (e.g. worry, fear), all of which may hinder communication. Besides, some institutional settings may create extremely sensitive and delicate conditions, sometimes even painful or antagonistic, making the client particularly vulnerable. On top of that, professionals such as doctors, nurses, police officers, social workers etc., are frequently in a hurry and expect the interpreters to deliver their services quickly and efficiently. Taking all of the above into consideration, community interpreters need people skills, as well as high linguistic and cultural competence, and since this type of interpreting is particularly demanding and emotionally challenging, the interpreter also needs to have particular interpersonal attributes such as trustworthiness, integrity and empathy (ibidem).

More details on the particular competences and skills required from interpreters will be provided in the following chapter.

---

18 https://web.archive.org/web/20090913071935/http://www.aiic.net/ViewPage.cfm/page234.htm#P5_365, accessed 12.02.2023.

Chapter 2:
Competences and Skills of Interpreters

2.1 Knowledge and Linguistic Skills

Whether consecutive, simultaneous, *a vista,* or community interpreters, they are always expected to deliver a professional service, hence the need to have particular skills and competences. Failure to perform well may result in misunderstandings or even in a breakdown in communication between interlocutors or linguistic groups. Therefore, it is necessary for professional interpreters to have skills that enable them to facilitate communication between participants in a multilingual context (Kalina 2000).[19]

Kalina (ibidem) observes that among the prerequisites for being a good interpreter are the linguistic skills which entail the knowledge of and a proficient command of two or more languages, as well as the ability to listen and speak at the same time. Linguistic skills include not only command of the general or conversational language, but also of specialized language varieties used in various areas (such as banking, medicine, technology, law, etc.). A skilled interpreter also needs to know the differences in use, style, register, cultural norms, and not only know them, but also be capable of handling them in various situations.

However, Kalina (ibidem) points out that it is not only the purely linguistic skills which are crucial in this profession, but also an extensive "knowledge of the cultures of the countries or regions concerned, including political, economic, social and ethnic differences, administrative structures, community life, but also literature and the arts". Professional interpreters also have to be familiar with the history, social developments, literature and political constitutions of all the countries of their working languages. This knowledge might be acquired by living and studying in the relevant countries for a certain period of time.

Also Horváth (2012, 44) stresses the importance of this cultural competence which is defined as the "ability to see the general behind the particular [...] and to establish rules with the aid of the individual incarnations" (Porcher 1988, after

---

19 https://core.ac.uk/download/pdf/41171576.pdf, accessed 13.02.2023.

Horváth 2012, 44). This means that in order to enable successful communication between people or groups belonging to different cultures, an interpreter needs to understand how those cultures operate. This necessitates the ability to see a bigger picture, i.e. to have a broad "view of the world that accommodates even those culture-bound behaviours, beliefs and representations that clash with one another and with [one's] culture(s) of origin" (Katan 2000, 241, after Horváth 2012, 45).

Cultural competence may also be referred to as "cross-cultural awareness" defined as "an awareness of the otherness and differentness of others, or rather of foreign cultures in all their complexity". This "presupposes the capacity for noticing, and, consequently, for understanding and tolerating the otherness of foreign cultures", as well as "it can prevent the automatic tendency to perceive the other and the different in terms of the known and the familiar" (Grosman 1994, 51, after Horváth 2012, 45). It also "promotes open-mindedness beyond one's own cultural border, contributing to a better understanding between people", and "constitutes an indispensable body of knowledge about the possibilities and relevance of differences between cultures" (ibidem).

Also various mental skills are essential in the interpreting profession. These entail, for instance, excellent memory and mnemonic capacity, the ability to work under pressure, high level of concentration, self-motivation, as well as tolerance to stress (Kalina 2000).

Kalina (ibidem) attempts to provide a definition of the interpreting competence, stating that:

> "[...] it refers to the ability to perform cognitive tasks of mediation within a bi-/ multilingual communication situation at an extremely high level of expectations and quality, often in a team of several interpreters. It includes the ability to interpret in the consecutive as well as simultaneous and any other mode such as whispering or dialogue interpreting. Interpreting takes place either between two languages (bilingual interpreting) or from one or several languages into one language which is generally the interpreter's mother tongue".

She also observes that since interpreters work in a wide variety of contexts and situations, the interpreting competence would also include comprehensive cultural and communication knowledge, a broad subject knowledge, as well as the ability to quickly broaden one's knowledge. Furthermore, skilled interpreters also need to be able to solve various linguistic, cultural, situational or other problems that may occur in the interpreting process, as well as always exhibit professional conduct, even when faced with difficulties arising in their work environment. They need to be flexible and able to adapt to technical challenges and ethical principles.

The above are certainly instances of extralinguistic skills and these, together with other required from a professional and competent interpreter, will be discussed in the following section.

2.2   Extralinguistic Skills

2.2.1   Memory

It goes without saying that interpreters need to have excellent memory skills so that they can remember details about the conversations or speeches they interpret, as the clients tend to rely on interpreters to relay information accurately and completely.

As stated by Horváth (2012, 203), memory is one of the most widely studied issues in interpreting studies. Phelan (2001, 4–5) asserts that "[t]he interpreter needs a good short-term memory to retain what he or she has just heard and a good long-term memory to put the information into context. Ability to concentrate is a factor as is the ability to analyze and process what is heard".

Zhong (2003)[20] provides a very approachable distinction between a short-term and a long-term memory stating that the former entails that one is "retaining information for a short period of time without creating the neural mechanisms for later recall", whereas the latter means that one has "created neural pathways for storing ideas and information which can then be recalled weeks, months, or even years later". In order to form these pathways, one needs to intentionally try to encode the information in the way they wish to recall it later. He also observes that the long-term memory is inextricably linked to an interpreter's learning process, one that constitutes an essential part of their acquisition of knowledge. This is due to the fact that the information stored in the long-term memory may last for minutes to weeks, months, or even an entire life, whereas the retention period of the short-term memory is a lot less than this, up to 30 seconds (Peterson 1959; Atkinson and Shiffrin 1968; Hebb 1949, after Zhong 2003). Memory in interpreting typically only lasts for a short time since once a particular interpreting task is finished, the interpreter moves on to another one, often involving a completely new context, subject and speakers (Zhong 2003).

While discussing memory in the interpreting profession, Horváth (2012, 203) refers to the model of memory during simultaneous interpretation of spoken languages proposed by Darò and Fabbro (1994) whereby "the source-language input is processed in the working memory and then sent to the functional system accounting for translation from L2 into L1 and from L1 into L2" (after Horváth

---

20 https://translationjournal.net/journal/25interpret.htm, accessed 19.02.2023.

2012, 203). What this entails and what actually happens is that verbal information is sent to the long-term memory systems which, in turn, send the necessary information to the translation systems. However, although this type of translation is called "simultaneous", the source language reception and the target language production do not actually happen at the same time; there is the so-called "lag", which is a certain amount of time that elapses between the point at which a unit of input reaches the interpreter's ear and the moment when he/she reproduces it in the target language (Shlesinger 2000, 40, after Horváth 2012, 205).

As regards the consecutive mode of interpreting, Gillies (2005, 109) states that good memory allows the interpreter to reduce the amount of notes they need to take while listening to the source language input, emphasizing at the same time that the principal role of notes is to be a form of an assistance and a prompt to memory which plays the most significant role. A similar stance is represented by Seleskovitch and Lederer (1989, after Horváth 2012, 206) who view note-taking as a tool that is supposed to facilitate concentration and analysis, with memory still being of paramount importance. Nevertheless, Mahmoodzadeh (1992, 234), while appreciating the role of memory in interpreting, states that in certain situations involving a substantial amount of linguistic material (including numbers, proper names, specialist terms, etc.), memory itself may prove insufficient and this is where note-taking comes especially in handy.[21]

Déjean Le Féal (1981, 76, after Tryuk 2007, 89) points out that during consecutive interpreting most of the memorization happens during the listening stage (due to the analysis of the cognitive content) and the actual reproduction of the text occurs long before the interpreter starts speaking. Regarding this memorization process, Ballester and Jimenez Hurtado (1992, 238–239) say that before storing the content of the speech in memory, the interpreter should first organize it into separate units of meaning, as this will allow them to process the individual utterance units. Then, during the interpretation, they need to process the message, using their memory. The interpreter should be able to isolate the units of meaning, arrange them in a way which would not only convey what is most important, but also maintain the logical structure and coherence of the original.

Horváth (2012, 206) draws the reader's attention to the link between memory and intelligence, referring to Seleskovitch and Lederer who state that the major difference between the two is that "while memory is responsible for the organisation and reorganisation of past experience, intelligence enables us to structure present experiences" (2002, 244–245, after Horváth 201, 206). Seleskovitch and Lederer also claim that instead of viewing memory and intelligence as opposite constructs, one should rather perceive them as complementary ones because

---

21 More information on note-taking for consecutive interpreting can be found in Chapter 3.

"[…] there is no intelligence without memory just as there is no engine without fuel and vice versa: storing elements in memory without any selection would condemn the mind to stagnation. In other words, one needs to select the important from the secondary, the relevant from the non-relevant" (ibidem).

Apart from memory, other vital extralinguistic skills of a professional interpreter are attention, focus and anticipation.

2.2.2 Attention, Focus and Anticipation

Pettersson (2001, 115) defines attention as the process of "selecting parts from all available sensory information, and from memorized information, for further mental processing".

According to Wickens and Carswell (2012, after Ashouri et al. 2021, 72), one may distinguish three modes of attention: selective attention, focused attention, and divided attention. The former entails selecting the information to be processed; focused attention means maintaining the processing of the information selected while at the same time excluding irrelevant input; and divided attention refers to the processing of more than one input at a given time.

Wickens et al. (2003, after Ashouri et al. 2021, 72–73) enumerate four factors affecting selective attention, which are: salience, expectancy, value, and effort. Salience means that certain features capture one's attention, and, according to these scholars, auditory stimuli are typically more salient than visual ones. Expectancy refers to the information about the probable time and place of knowledge accessibility, whereas value is the importance of the information as well as awareness that knowledge serves practical functions. Finally, effort is a negative factor and is involved in moving attention from one portion of information to another.

Horváth (2012, 207) observes that attention plays a significant role in executing complex cognitive tasks and interpreting may be regarded as one such task. Other scholars, such as Darò et al. (1996, 102), express a similar view, adding that attention is crucial in the process of memorization of verbal input and unless attention is focused on the task, the short-term memory may be disrupted. Attention also plays an essential role in the process of long-term verbal memorization. Liu (2008) claims that the interpreter's attention must be directed to the pieces of information so that they produce more significant amount of data. If the interpreter fails to focus on the chunks of data, the end result might be disorganized and confusing (after Ashouri et al. 2021, 74).

In their studies regarding attention in interpreting, Darò et al. (1996) found that during simultaneous interpretation, focusing conscious attention on the input or on the output does not influence the interpreter's general performance. Nevertheless, the scholars point out to one exception: in the process of active interpretation from the source language into the target language the interpreters may find it helpful to focus their attention on the output "[...] since this may help them to reduce false starts, pauses, hesitations, corrections, additions and morphosyntactic mistakes" (1996, 101).

The need to focus on the output is also emphasized by Camayd-Freixas (2011, 12) who states that comprehension (i.e. listening) is predominantly passive in terms of mental processing, whereas production (i.e. speaking) requires more attention. Therefore, he suggests that during simultaneous interpreting more attentional resources are allocated to the production side. However, he also points out that once the formulation phase is over, which means that the interpreter has already decided what to say, the delivering phase becomes mostly automatic and the interpreter's attention could switch back to listening.

Apart from attention and focus, which are indispensable for successful interpreting performance, another factor that plays an enormous role is anticipation. Horváth (2012, 209) claims that anticipation is one of the most important strategies in interpreting.

While discussing anticipation, Chernov (1994) refers to the idea of redundancy within which he distinguishes two types: objective and subjective, both of which, as he claims, "[...] allow for, and indeed, signify the predictability of meaning and sense in the message" (Chernov 1994, 145). Objective redundancy, also called textual redundancy, depends on the message recipient and entails repetition of the message components. Total redundancy of a text, on the other hand, is higher than the level of its objective redundancy because the extra redundancy "[...] arises from interaction between the semantic structure of a discourse in progress and the cognitive store of the hearer, i. e. her knowledge of the world in general, or her familiarity with ("background knowledge" about) the present communication situation" (Chernov 2004, 57, after Horváth 2012, 210). Within his redundancy model, Chernov also proposes a hierarchy of speech levels on the basis of which one may assess the anticipation mechanism in simultaneous interpretation and these are as follows: syllable – word – syntagm – utterance – discourse. As he further states, along these levels the interpreter anticipates the message development and redundancy may be traced at each of these speech levels (ibidem).

As for the notion of subjective redundancy, Chernov (2004) explains it by referring to yet another term, namely: inference. Whenever one is listening to someone, he/she makes inferences about the message on the following levels: linguistic, cognitive, situational and pragmatic. The predominant objective of inferencing is understanding and, whether in day-to-day communication, or in interpreting, inferencing is a fast and subconscious process, but this is only when "the redundancy of the message is sufficiently high. With low redundancy, comprehension is hampered and slowed" (2004, 60). As the scholar points out, comprehension starts when the listener is capable of making an inference from the part of the message that has already been conveyed, through his/her perception of the incoming semantic components and relating them to:

- "other semantic components and their configurations in the discourse (linguistic inference);
- elements in [his/]her long-term memory or thesaurus of world knowledge (cognitive inference);
- factors in the situational context of the discourse (deictic and situational inference);
- the social role of the speaker (pragmatic inference)" (ibidem).

Referring back to the notion of anticipation, Chernov considers it as the basic cognitive process enabling one to perform simultaneous interpretation. He further explains that anticipation is largely determined by the level of text redundancy, claiming that "the higher the redundancy of the discourse, the higher the probability of correct anticipation of its development at each level. The reverse is also true: the higher the information density of the discourse [...], the lower the probability of correctly forecasting its development" (Chernov 2004, 93).

However, one should remember that all those speech levels of message development are interdependent and either all or several of them, whether at the same time or in sequence, are involved in the perception and comprehension of the source language message, which, in turn, allows the interpreter to transfer the message into the target language (Chernov 2004, 171).

As neatly summed up by Horváth (2012, 212), anticipation of the message development is one of the basic mental operations in interpreting, "[i]t operates at a hierarchy of speech levels and depends, to a large extent, on the objective and subjective redundancy of the discourse as well as on the interpreter's inferencing ability".

Apart from the already discussed factors of memory, attention, focus and anticipation, there is yet another issue worth raising when speaking about interpreter's extralinguistic skills and that is stress management.

2.2.3 Managing Occupational Stress

2.2.3.1 Occupational Stress and its Components

As pointed out by Horváth (2012, 156), these days stress is not necessarily perceived as something negative. Quite the contrary, it is frequently seen as a potential tool to mobilize one's inner resources, leading, in turn, to better performance, regardless of the area one wishes to perform in. Nevertheless, the scholar (ibidem) observes that stress may still be damaging to one's mental and physical health if one fails to learn how to tackle it. The ability to do so predominantly depends on one's personality, as well as the conscious effort to control stressful situations.

As regards stress management in general, and stress during language interpreting in particular, it is crucial, as observed by Horváth (2012, 155), to become "stress literate", which means "to understand stress, recognise its symptoms and come up with one's own tailor-made stress management techniques".

When discussing stress and, in particular, possible reactions to it, Horváth (2012, 155–156) refers to the division proposed by Zeier (1997) who distinguished between active and passive coping behaviour in response to stress. The former consists of the fight or flight response, where both responses are linked to physical activation. Further, as Zeier (1997, 232–233, after Horváth 2012, 155–156) states:

> "[s]ituations which engender in us the fear of losing control usually elicit some active coping behaviour. However, if one loses control and does not know which active behaviour to select for managing a stressful situation, [...] passive coping occurs. This response may range from avoidance behaviour, resignation, feelings of inferiority and lack of self-confidence to severe depression".

As claimed by Zeier (1997, 233–234), these two coping mechanisms are related to two physiological stress response systems: the Cannon stress-axis and the Selye stress-axis. The symptoms of the former are increased "blood pressure, heart rate, respiration cycle, metabolic rate, muscle activity and electrodermal activity" and decreased "saliva secretion and [...] the temperature of the fingers and hands. Furthermore, energy stores are tapped and stored sugars and lipids are released into the blood stream. This physiological response [...] prepares the organism to perform physical work".

Zeier (1997, 233) states that the Selye stress-axes "stimulates the secretion of the adrenocortical hormones, in particular the stress hormone cortisol". The scholar also points out to yet another type of possible stress reaction: the one which occurs in stressful situations when one decides to resort to a passive behaviour. He states that this may result in certain vegetative stress symptoms such as "an upset stomach, vomiting or diarrhoea, and in the long run ulcers and other gastrointestinal diseases" (1997, 234).

When discussing stress in the interpreting profession, Horváth (2012, 157) says that "[s]tress is and has been for some time a widely researched topic in interpreting studies for it seems to be a fact of life for interpreters". He also states that most of the literature on this topic concerns simultaneous interpreting, because, perhaps, this is the most frequently used mode of interpreting in international institutions hiring the highest number of interpreters, like the UN or the EU (ibidem). However, as the scholar rightly observes, this by no means implies that "the other types of interpreting are linguistically or contextually less complex, nor are they less stressful by nature. A professional situation can be perceived as threatening by consecutive or community interpreters as well, and they can be uncertain about how to cope with it, too" (ibidem).

Generally speaking, stress consists of the psychophysiological processes caused by a perceived threat or danger. From a psychological point of view, stress has two components:
- the experience of a threatening and strenuous situation;
- the uncertainty whether one is able to cope with this situation.

Among the stressors one may distinguish the following: environmental (noise, heat etc.), mental (tasks requiring attention over longs periods of time, decision making etc.) and stressors related to interactions with colleagues, superiors and subordinates etc. (Kurz 1983, cited in AIIC[22] Workload Study 2002, 6).

The same scholar defines occupational or job stress "the harmful physical and emotional responses that occur when the requirements of the job do not match the capabilities, resources or needs of the worker" (Kurz 2003, 51), at the same time pointing out that this kind of stress is frequently related to psychological distress and a negative impact on one's health. Stress can have "disruptive after-effects, including persistent physiological arousal, psychological distress, reduced task performance, and, over time, declines in cognitive capabilities" (Tayler, 1995, 254, in Riccardi et al., 1998, cited in AIIC Workload Study 2002, 7).

When discussing occupational stress within the interpreting profession, Horváth (2012, 157) also refers to the AIIC Workload Study, which recognized three crucial factors affecting how stressful the interpretation process might be for the interpreters, and these are as follows:

---

22 International Association of Conference Interpreters – an organization established in 1953 with a view to promoting the highest standards of quality and ethics in interpreting (more information on the AIIC can be found at: https://aiic.org/).

- psychological parameters (perception, attitudes, etc.);
- physical parameters of working conditions (i. e. air quality, noise insulation, lighting, etc. in booths);
- physiological parameters (heart rate, blood pressure, cortisol level, etc.) (AIIC Workload Study 2002, 3–4).[23]

However, as aptly noticed by Horváth (2012, 157–158), it appears that the latter ones, i. e. physiological parameters like increased heart rate and blood pressure, are consequences of stress rather than factors affecting the stressfulness of a situation, and they should rather be perceived as good measurement tools allowing one to assess whether (and if so, to what degree) a given situation is stressful for the interpreter.

Nevertheless, the AIIC Workload Study provides a list of factors related to the physical working environment, which are perceived by the interpreters as contributing most to their occupational stress and, in turn, negatively affecting their performance and job satisfaction. The list concerns simultaneous interpreting in particular and enumerates the following work-related stressors:
- difficulties related to delivery and text (this may mean, for instance, speakers who speak very fast or read from texts, texts that are very complex, poorly delivered texts, etc.) – interpretation is not only about the purely linguistic elements and the message behind them, but also about intonation, voice quality, changes in pitch and loudness, pauses, as well as non-verbal aspects like gestures, facial expressions, etc., all of which contribute to the message (Stenzl 1983, cited in AIIC Workload Study 2002, 7–8). The manner in which the speaker delivers their speech significantly affects the comfort level of the interpreter and, in turn, his/her performance. For instance, it is the speaker and the speed at which they deliver their speech that dictates the pace of interpreting and, unfortunately, the interpreter is unable to control this aspect. What is more, since it is impossible for interpreters to be experts in all the subject matters discussed during conferences, they frequently have no choice but to work with an information deficit in relation to the speakers. This entails that they need to make assumptions about the information they are going to receive and may encounter serious problems if their assumptions turn out to be incorrect (ibidem). Yet another factor belonging to this group of work-related stress factors, and one over which interpreters have no control, is how spontaneous or prepared the speech is. Spontaneous speech, or unscripted texts, are frequently chaotic, repetitive, often with a high redundancy level. In contrast, prepared and semi-prepared texts tend to be structured, more sys-

---

23 https://aiic.org/document/468/aiicwebzine_febmar2002_7_aiic_interpreter_wo, accessed 25.02.2023.

tematic and consciously organized (Nida 1964, cited in AIIC Workload Study 2002, 8);

- increased time on task – AIIC Workload Study (ibidem) quotes the results of another study, conducted by Moser-Mercer et al. (1998), which investigated the effect of increased time on task on physiological and psychological stress and on performance. The experiment involved 5 experienced conference interpreters, who worked for 30 minutes, then rested for 3 minutes and then continued working for the next 50 minutes after which they had a 2-minute break. After analyzing the results, it was concluded that the participants were experiencing an increase in stress-related emotions (such as anxiety, depression, aggressiveness) during the first 30 minutes and, as time on task was increasing, they were feeling more and more overloaded, and, as a result, they were more likely to exhibit the "I couldn't care less" attitude;
- inadequate visibility of speaker and/or audience – since human communication involves both verbal and non-verbal aspects, interpreters rely not only on signals received through the auditory channel, but also through the visual one. Hence, it is important that both the speaker and the audience are clearly visible (Cooper et al. 1982, cited in AIIC Workload Study 2002, 8). As the stages of analysis and understanding appear to play a crucial role in the process of interpretation, the interpreter needs to acquire as much information as possible in order to deliver a successful performance, and here non-verbal signal might be particularly useful. AIIC Workload Study (2002, 8–9) provides an example to illustrate the significance of non-verbal cues:

> "For instance, in order to avoid being surprised by an unexpected speaker or by a switch of language, the interpreter has to rely exclusively on visual information (changes in gaze direction, recognition of a speaker by the chair, etc.)".

As claimed by Riccardi et al. (1998, cited in AIIC Workload Study 2002, 9), it appears that when the interpreter has no visual contact with the speaker and/ or the audience, this causes a greater dependence on verbal elements, as well as demands greater concentration on the linguistic aspects of the speech, which, in turn, may generate a more stressful situation for the interpreter and may lead to an impaired performance;

- physical working conditions (for example: high level of humidity, not enough fresh air, uncomfortable temperature, inadequate lighting, background noise, uncomfortable seating, etc.) – all these may seriously affect the interpreters' physical comfort. On the basis of interviews with 33 interpreters in Europe (Cooper et. al. 1982, cited in AIIC Workload Study 2002, 10), the following physical environmental factors were reported as the main sources of stress:

- inadequate ventilation (insufficient amount of fresh air may cause discomfort, and too low air velocity may lead to lethargy and drowsiness);
- excessive or poor lighting ("illumination level is the amount of light cast on a certain indoor surface from a natural or artificial source of light. Illumination levels are usually measured on work surfaces");
- too small booths (this factor is also connected with higher temperatures contributing to the general discomfort);
- incorrect use of microphones (for instance, speakers talking too close to the microphone, or several microphones being turned on at the same time);
- background noise (noise above a certain level for a certain amount of time is harmful to the human ear. Also noise that is of a lower level may have a negative impact on the productivity and the person's comfort since it constitutes "nuisance" noise);
- uncomfortable seating (affecting neck and back);
- preparation difficulties (the need to spend long hours preparing for a specific subject-area; the situation when the preparation material is unavailable in advance).

According to the study, among these factors, the interpreters listed the condition of the booth as the most stressful one, followed by difficulties in text and delivery. However, even though the study concerns simultaneous interpreting, the majority of its findings are certainly applicable to other interpreting modes as well (for instance, visibility, text delivery, textual complexity, temperature, preparation difficulties, etc.).

Nevertheless, occupational stress experienced by interpreters does not only concern strictly physical factors, but also other aspects. On the basis of interviews with interpreters, and a mail survey among AIIC members, the following categories were distinguished (Cooper et al. 1982; AIIC Workload Study 2002, 11–12): task related factors, interpersonal factors, home/work interface, organizational/management, and subjective.

1. Task-related factors:
   - high levels of concentration and information overload;
   - extended work periods and long workdays;
   - inconsiderate speakers or organizers (for instance, material is not provided to interpreters in advance; speakers deliver their presentation too fast; the material is read rather than spoken; "poor interpretation" is used as an excuse for underlying political disagreements; speech is delivered in a non-native language and might be difficult to interpret due to incoherence or to a non-native accent);
   - incompetent speakers;
   - the necessity to spend a lot of time preparing for a specific subject;

- lack of significant career advancement and of official recognition;
- erratic schedules, sudden changes in assignments;
- evaluation by senior interpreters, or a complete lack of evaluation or feedback on performance.
2. Interpersonal factors:
    - relationships with colleagues – uncooperative colleagues, competition for jobs (particularly among freelancers);
    - relationships with superiors or organizers – fear of rejecting too many jobs in a row, and the need to maintain a good relationship with the organizers.
3. Home/work interface factors:
    - personal problems affecting interpreters' performance and their overall work;
    - frequent travel and long absences, which may be an obstacle to family and social life.
4. Subjective (emotional) factors:
    - interpreters admitted to feeling responsible for the result of the conference and reported the feeling of job insecurity.

As regards the burnout syndrome, it has been found that the level of burnout of the interpreters is higher than among hi-tech employees, which allows one to conclude that interpreters experience a high level of this particular syndrome (Horváth 2012, 160). And just as, as previously discussed, the interpreters are likely to adopt the "I couldn't care less attitude" as the time on task increases, they are prone to doing so in any situation "where they have to exceed their personal limits" (Moser-Mercer and Künzli 1995, after Zeier 1997, 246). This might be considered a defence mechanism which, as pointed out by Mouzourakis (1996, after Horváth 2012, 160), is employed by interpreters in highly stressful situations and whereby they are "[…] progressively reducing their efforts, even to the point of adopting an automatic pilot mode". This, in turn, allows them to achieve "stress homeostasis" (ibidem). This might be regarded as a passive coping response to stress due to mental overload, and is particularly visible in situations when one does not have the mental (or physical) resources to respond actively (ibidem).

Long-term exposure to work-related stressors can take a toll on one's body and mental health, causing anxiety and depression and, in some cases, leading to serious mental health problems. Studies have demonstrated that younger people who are regularly burdened with heavy workloads and time pressure at work are more likely to develop depression or an anxiety disorder. Besides, high levels of stress can affect physical health, as constant activation of the fight-or-flight response may increase the organism's susceptibility to disease and the repeated release of cortisol may affect the immune system, leading a person to develop autoimmune disorders, cardiovascular disease, and Alzheimer's disease. It may also negatively affect one's exercise, eating habits, and sleep.[24]

Although one may claim that interpreters are professionals who have chosen this job consciously and intentionally, and so they should be well-aware that it entails, as illustrated above, a high level of both physiological and psychological stress, this does not mean that they should be left to their own devices when trying to handle it. On the contrary, they should be aware that they have a wide range of tools at their disposal that would allow them to combat the negative effects of stress related to their occupation and, in time, become much more resistant to this kind of stress.

2.2.3.2 Management of Occupational Stress

Occupational stress is something that has been proven to remain constant throughout one's career, which means that it is experienced not only by novice interpreters, but also professional ones find their job stressful, too. However, the results of the research on the occupational stress within the interpreting profession have demonstrated that "the level of stress tends to decrease with experience during [the interpreters'] career" (Horváth 2012, 159). This may be partially due to the fact that competence and motivation "modify the association between stress and performance", and "highly competent [and motivated] workers are more likely to maintain a high level of performance even in the face of stressors" (AIIC Workload Study 2002, cited in Horváth 2012, 159). Hence, it appears that experience and competence can be of great assistance as regards handling stress during interpreting. It also seems that the more experienced interpreters, when faced with stressful situations, also more likely to use certain coping techniques such as mental control and attention focusing techniques. This indicates an active, rather than passive, response to stress (Boronkay-Roe 2006, after Horváth 2012, 160).

Obviously, the perception of something as dangerous (hence causing stress) is also determined by one's personality. As stated by Horváth (2012, 159), the extent to which individuals experience a factor that has a stressful effect on them or their work depends on their level of self-confidence and self-knowledge. This, in turn, has a favourable impact on their ability to tackle the situation. Interestingly enough, the findings of the mail survey conducted revealed that about 50% of the interpreters perceived their work-related stress as useful and positive, whereas 30% saw it as negative (AIIC Workload Study 2002, 122).

---

24 https://www.health.harvard.edu/blog/how-to-handle-stress-at-work-2019041716436, accessed 28.02.2023.

AIIC Workload Study (2002, 129–131) includes certain recommendations regarding the issue of handling occupational stress within the interpreting profession (and these concern not only the interpreters themselves, but also the speakers, the organizers, as well as the superiors):

1. In order to reduce stress caused by poor speech delivery and text complexity, it is recommended that the speakers use their native language if only interpreting from this particular language is possible. This will reduce the risk of "poor delivery" due to a foreign accent. Also, the speakers should be encouraged to minimize their reading of pre-scripted speeches (this is of particular importance if the interpreter had no prior access to the text).
2. To minimize stress related to the interpreter's insufficient preparation, it is recommended that the written texts of speeches are distributed in advance together with any background material such as minutes of prior meetings, etc., as well as any relevant conference material (such as agenda).
3. If the quality of the delivery deteriorates in the course of the presentation, it is advisable that both the interpreters and conference organizers have agreed in advance on a signal indicating difficulty in interpretation. This signal has to be visible and needs to be respected by the speakers, allowing the time for explanation and improvement of delivery.
4. As regards the work schedule, the interpreters would find it helpful if they were provided information on the incoming assignments in advance (the more so if the venue is remote), as this would give them time for the necessary preparations, including technical aspects.
5. As for the level of comfort in the booths, they should be large enough to accommodate the necessary number of interpreters. According to the International Association of Conference Interpreters (AIIC),[25] the size of a booth is governed by the need to provide sufficient work space and air volume per interpreter. The minimum number of interpreters per booth is two and the AIIC demands the following minimum booth dimensions:
   - width: 2.50 m
   - depth: 2.40 m
   - height: 2.30 m
   Also the air supply and air quality affect the comfort in the booth. According to ISO recommendations (cited in AIIC Workload Study 2002, 130), airflow into the booths should be exchanged at a rate of at least 7 times per hour and the air supply should contain 100% fresh air. The booths should also be equipped with temperature and humidity regulators that should be regularly maintained. The ventilation system should be turned on approximately one

---

25 https://aiic.org/document/4385/ISO%202603%20-%20fixed%20booths%20for%20simultan eous%20interpretation%20-%20ENG.pdf, accessed 27.02.2023.

hour before the beginning of the conference, and left on continuously throughout the day. The system should also be as silent as possible.

Since the levels of lighting in the booths may also generate certain problems, for instance light being reflected from the booth's window, which could, in turn, negatively affect the interpreter's vision when a conference room is dark, the following recommendations have been formulated (AIIC Workload Study 2002, 131):

– providing table lamps;
– installing mirrored windows in the booths.

The above detailed recommendations have been formulated with a view to reducing occupational stress of interpreters. Nevertheless, there is a wide range of very general tips of how to better handle stress at work, regardless of the profession, and these could also be found useful and be successfully applied by interpreters, whether novice or experienced ones:[26]

1. Recognize your stressors – try to identify the situations which cause you most stress; this may be done in writing: you may record your thoughts, feelings, as well as details about the environment in those particular situations. For instance, for several days you may record the situations, circumstances and people who cause you to react in a negative way, including a brief description of each situation, answering questions such as:
    – Where were you?
    – Who was involved?
    – What was your reaction?
    – How did you feel?
    – What are the ways of resolving it?
    Taking such notes might be helpful in identifying certain patters among your stressors as well as your reactions to them.

2. Develop healthy responses – you may, for instance, practise sport or engage in any other form of physical activity like going for a walk. Spending time on your hobbies and activities you like may also prove excellent for relieving stress. Also making sure you get good quality sleep is important for effective

---

26 The list of recommendations regarding stress management has been compiled on the basis of the following sources: https://www.apa.org/topics/healthy-workplaces/work-stress; https://www.mind.org.uk/information-support/tips-for-everyday-living/how-to-be-mentally-healthy-at-work/work-and-stress/; https://www.verywellmind.com/how-to-deal-with-stress-at-work-3145273, https://www.mayoclinic.org/healthy-lifestyle/stress-management/in-depth/coping-with-stress/art-20048369; https://www.health.harvard.edu/blog/how-to-handle-stress-at-work-2019041716436; https://www.healthline.com/health/work-stress; https://www.forbes.com/health/mind/how-to-deal-with-stress-at-work/, accessed 27.02.2023.

stress management and this might be facilitated by limiting the caffeine intake and avoiding stimulating activities at night.

3. Set boundaries – nowadays people often feel pressure to be available around the clock, due to omnipresent technology. Hence it is very important to establish certain work-life boundaries, for instance not checking email from home in the evening or not answering work-related calls during days off or holidays. Creating boundaries between one's personal and professional life can significantly reduce stress.

4. Reset and recharge – in order to avoid chronic stress and prevent burnout, it is necessary to find time to be able to return to the pre-stress level. This entails finding moments in which you are not involved in any work-related activities or thinking about work. Focus on your life outside work by nurturing relationships with friends and pursuing interests unconnected with your work. These periods of "switching off" and "disconnecting" from work-related issues help to reduce the stress level and restore one's mental balance.

5. Learn to relax and unwind – there is a wide range of relaxation techniques that you may try, such as yoga, meditation, deep breathing exercises, visualization, mindfulness ("an ability to be fully present, aware of where we are and what we're doing, and not overly reactive or overwhelmed by what's going on around us").[27] This practice is about focusing on the here and now. It might help you to find calmness and clarity to respond to stressful situations. You may start by trying to focus for a few minutes on a simple activity like breathing, walking, or enjoying a meal. With time, you will notice you become less and less distracted while doing so and you will be able to use this ability in many areas of your life.

6. Work on your time management – if you feel overwhelmed or under pressure at work, improving your time management may prove helpful. Sometimes, feeling overwhelmed by work comes down to how organized you are. You can start by setting realistic goals and expectations and then making a priority list of tasks. If a certain task or project is particularly complex and difficult, it is useful to break it into smaller steps to be completed gradually. You can also overcome procrastination by setting assigning time blocks for deep concentration work.

7. Avoid multitasking – once highly praised as a way of maximizing one's productivity, multitasking is no longer considered that affective. In fact, a lot of people realize that when doing several things at the same time, their speed and accuracy suffer. Therefore, instead of multitasking, a much more effective technique might be "chunking", which means setting aside "chunks of time to focus on one specific task while minimizing interruptions, and

---

27 https://www.mindful.org/what-is-mindfulness/, accessed 28.02.2023.

grouping similar tasks together (like checking all email at once rather than throughout the day)."[28] As a result, greater focus and efficiency are achieved.

8. Let go of perfectionism – while it definitely has certain benefits, perfectionism can be highly stressful and lead to burnout. Therefore, try to focus on the effort you put into a task instead of personalizing failure when you make a mistake.

9. Reward yourself for achievements – give yourself some small and simple rewards for completed tasks, such as taking a break to read, listen to your favourite music, play a game or spend time outside.

10. Talk to your supervisor – since healthy employees mean increased productivity, managers should be keen to promote healthy work environment and prioritize well-being of employees. Therefore, an honest conversation with your supervisor may lead to establishing an effective plan for managing the stressors. Solutions might include, for instance, improving time management, getting the necessary resources or support from colleagues, or introducing changes to your physical workspace to make it more comfortable.

11. Get support – help from friends and family members can significantly reduce one's stress. Support and assistance may also be available at your workplace in the form of special programs for employees or counselling. Having people you can rely on during the tough times can alleviate some of the built-up tension.

12. Seek professional counselling – the belief that only people suffering from mental conditions need therapy is a myth. Feeling overwhelmed at work is a good reason to reach out for professional help and support. Working with a professional psychotherapist can offer an outlet for your frustrations, it can also help you better identify your stressors at work, as well as provide healthy coping mechanisms. A professional may also assist you in developing strategies for "disconnecting" and taking care of yourself.

Since the profession of an interpreter certainly belongs to stressful ones, one should never neglect the psychological aspects of the interpreting practice. It seems obvious that exposure to stress may make it more difficult for an interpreter, whether a novice or an experienced one, to perform effectively and, as a result, may lead to decreased quality of interpreting output. Also, anxiety experienced by interpreters may significantly hinder their performance. Hence it is so important for interpreters to, first of all, recognize their stress triggers, and, secondly, to learn how to effectively cope with them.

---

28 https://www.verywellmind.com/single-tasking-for-productivity-and-stress-management-3144753, accessed 28.02.2023.

Stress has been, and will always be, an inherent part of an interpreting practice and a constant companion of every practising interpreter. Apart from being aware of the stressors and learning effective coping mechanisms, it is also experience, competence, and confidence that help to handle difficult situations in the courtroom and other interpretation settings. Although the above-mentioned tips are definitely of invaluable help, being a successful interpreter requires more than effective stress management: it also demands a particular personality, courage, a desire to serve others, and the willingness to manage stressful situations and strong emotions.

While moderate amount of stress for a short period of time may actually be beneficial in the interpreting profession, as it mobilizes the interpreter's autonomic nervous system and sharpens his/her senses, thus helping them to think and act quickly, chronic stress for an extended period of time can cause tightness in the body, shortness of breath, decline in brain function, and lack of energy, all of which translates to decreased enthusiasm and motivation for work and life in general. Therefore, it is imperative for the interpreter to be able to identify the factors that stress him/her and address them effectively. There are a lot of strategies to apply (such as the ones discussed above), but the key for every single interpreter is to commit themselves to finding what works specifically for them, as this, in the long run, will significantly increase their job satisfaction as well as the overall quality of life.

Chapter 3:
Note-Taking in Interpreting

3.1 The Role and Principles of Note-Taking

As mentioned in the previous chapter, interpreters are expected to have much more than just language skills. Besides having a proficient command of the target language, they should also have a thorough knowledge and mastery of their own language and culture, as well as the cultures of the foreign language or languages with which they work.

Another crucial skill that every good interpreter needs to master is the skill of note-taking. As stated by Kohn and Albl-Mikasa (2002, 257): "Consecutive interpreting is typically used for press conferences, after-dinner speeches and similar occasions. The statements to be interpreted can be as long as 20 minutes. As the capacity of the human memory is insufficient to provide a consecutive of longer statements, the interpreters make notes to support their memory and thus to facilitate the rendition in the target language".

Rozan (2002, 73) observes that a lot of people claim that consecutive interpreting cannot be learned and the notes the interpreters take depend to a significant degree on the interpreter's personality. However, Rozan (ibidem) disagrees with this opinion, stating that his own years-long experience in interpreting suggests the opposite. Whereas he agrees that there are some prerequisites that a good interpreter should meet, such as an extensive general knowledge, a proficient command of the languages between which one is interpreting, "flexibility" in both languages, as well as adaptability to the situation, he asserts that the skill of note-taking is absolutely trainable and can be learned. Therefore, he proposed a system of note-taking for consecutive interpreting, formulating 7 rules and introducing 20 symbols together with a plethora of examples how to use them in the interpreting practice. Nevertheless, Rozan (ibidem) clearly states that every single interpreter should preserve his/her own personality and, therefore, the system that he proposed by no means should by copied automatically and uncritically. It should rather serve as an inspiration and every single interpreter or interpreting trainee should select those elements of it that they consider most fitting, and adapt them to their individual needs and individual interpreting contexts and situations.

The most general idea behind note-taking for consecutive interpreting is jotting down the main points of the source language speech, as well as all the necessary connectors, in a manner that would serve as a memory support for reproducing the target language speech. For the interpreter it is crucial to note down ideas or concepts rather than entire words, and the interpreter should remember that the notes are to be memory triggers, rather than words substitution. Therefore, dedicating an excessive effort and amount of time on trying to write down the entire discourse tends to prove futile. Instead, the interpreter should only note down the necessary ideas or key words that will help them with the reformulation of the speech.

Since there is no universally-used system of note-taking or symbols for the purpose of consecutive interpreting, every single interpreter is typically encouraged to develop their own note-taking system based on their own experience and needs, adjusted to the given situation they have to tackle. Their own individual note-taking system should be one that they find helpful and are comfortable with, as well as the notes should be organized and easy to understand.

The essential aspect that is indispensable for producing good notes is selectivity. This entails adapting the role of the audience and carefully selecting the most crucial information from the speech to be later on rendered into the target language. At the same time, the notes should be written and structured in such a way so as to successfully trigger the interpreter's memory.[29]

Also, one needs to remember that notes are short-lived and are effective only when used within minutes after the speech has finished since the speech is still fresh in the memory of the interpreter and, with the assistance of notes, they are capable of interpreting what has just been said. Notes are also personal and so they can only be used by the very interpreter who took them, as for other interpreters they may be totally meaningless.

Professional interpreters tend to offer the following advice on the note-taking:[30]

– one should take notes quickly, without waiting for the "right" word as there is simply no time for that;
– one should write down words that are easy to understand in order to later trigger one's memory when one has to render the speech into the target language;

29 https://smartidiom.pt/en/note-taking-in-consecutive-interpreting-too-muchtoo-little-how-and-what-to-note-take/, accessed 12.03.2023.
30 Ibidem.

- one should avoid using loose pages and should opt for notepads in order to facilitate organization of notes, preferably using one side of the page only and writing in large letters so that they are visible from a larger distance;
- when interpreting the speech one should always keep an eye contact with the audience;
- one should avoid using ambiguous abbreviations which means that one particular abbreviation should always have the same meaning, regardless of the interpreting situation;
- one should use either the existing symbols or the symbols that are already easily recognizable and meaningful to them instead of trying to invent symbols ad hoc during the speech.

Since the writing speed is always slower than the speaking speed, it is impossible for the interpreter to write down everything that the speaker says. Hence, the interpreter needs to be able to identify, select and note down the most important ideas and elements but omit anything which is not relevant to the understanding of the speech. Most professional interpreters agree that the information to be written down in the form of notes should include the following:[31]
- introduction and conclusion;
- the main ideas (by recording them it is later much easier for the interpreter to trace back the structure of the speech and preserve the original content in translation);
- links between ideas, which may be done using connectors, as these help the interpreter to establish a logical sequence of ideas (the logical consequence might be expressed with words *consequently, as a result, accordingly* or *therefore*; the logical cause might be conveyed with the words *because, due to, as,* or *since*; and the opposition – by means of the words *but, yet, however or nevertheless*; sample linking words used for note-taking are presented in Table 1 below);

1.	effect -> cause		cos
because, the main reason for this, what is causing this, what's behind this?			
2.	cause -> effect		so
hence, this means that, the result of this is, the consequence of this is, so that			
3.	so we can conclude, therefore, this would suggest that, thus		⟶⟶⟶>
because, the main reason for this, what is causing this, what's behind this?			
4.	purpose, objective		to
(in order) to, in such a way as to, so that, with the aim of, the purpose being to,			

31 https://smartidiom.pt/en/note-taking-in-consecutive-interpreting-too-muchtoo-little-how-and-what-to-note-take/; https://studfile.net/preview/5650192/, accessed 12.03.2023.

5.	following limit, contradiction			but
however, nonetheless, on the other hand, in spite of this				
6.	preceding limit, contradiction			tho
although, despite (the fact that), even though				
7.	condition and consequence			if
if .....then... (or inversion of same), had I known, were this to happen				
8.	question			wot, wen, y, wer, who, ?
9.	in addition			+
also, in addition, and, not only, on top of that there is,				
10.	NO LINK			‖

Table 1. Sample linking words used in note-taking for consecutive interpreting (source: https://studfile.net/preview/5650192/page:3/, accessed 12.03.2023).

- keywords;
- opinions and points of view;
- noncontextualized information, i.e. elements which cannot be recalled on the basis of analytical and logical thinking in a given context; these elements include, for instance: numbers, proper names, dates, names of days and months, lists of things and terms; they need to be noted down as they typically do not evoke any associations in the interpreter and so they tend to be quickly forgotten;
- technical terms, terminology;
- the tense (the present, the past, the future), the mode and the conditional, as these largely affect the meaning; one way of recording them is to put a graphic sign near the verb form. For instance, "ll" sign will indicate the future, a "d" sign will show the past, a circumflexed stress ∧ will show the conditional, whereas no extra sign will be used for the present tense, for example:

We say	we ‖ 0
We said	we ‖ d
We will say	we ‖ -ll
We would say	we ‖ ∧
He likes to work:	he ♥ wk 0
He is living in the States	He liv. usa

As for modal verbs, they may conveniently be written in English, since they tend to be short: *may, must, can, want,* etc. or *should = shd; could = cd; would = ∧; must = › ; may = may.*

When note-taking, professional interpreters also use all sorts of shortenings and abbreviations, typically applying two basic techniques, i.e. clipping and graphical abbreviations.

Clipping entails that the word is formed from the syllable of the original word, which may lose its beginning, its ending, both the beginning and the ending, its central part, or the whole form of the word may be transformed, this may happen as a result of the following mechanisms:[32]

- aphaeresis – the process where the word loses its beginning, e. g.: *phone* (telephone), *bus* (omnibus, autobus), *cycle* (bicycle), *copter* (helicopter), *car* (motor-car), *coon* (raccoon), *cola* (coca-cola), etc.;
- apocope – the process where the word loses its ending, e. g.: *exam* (examination), *prof* (professor), *vac* (vacation), *lab* (laboratory), *alg* (algebra), *algo* (algorithm), *ad* (advertisement), *admin* (administrator, administration), *cab* (cabriolet), *lib* (liberty, liberation), *gym* (gymnasium, gymnastics), *cert* (certificate, certainly), *demo* (demonstration), *movie* (moving-picture), *Oct.* (October), *perm* (permanent wave), *pop* (from popular music, art, singer) etc.;
- the word loses both its beginning and ending, e. g.: *fridge* (refrigerator), *flu* (influenza), *tec* (detective) etc.;
- syncope – the process where the word loses its central part, e. g.: *circs* (circumstances), *conds* (conditions), *pants* (pantaloons), *combs* (combination garments), *specs* (spectacles, specifications), *maths* (from mathematics) *Dr.* (doctor), *Mr.* (mister), *St* (saint), etc.;
- the entire form of the word is transformed, e. g.: *Mrs.* (mistress, missis), *Xmas* (Christmas), *bike* (bicycle), *nightie* (nightdress), *hanky* (handkerchief), *mike* (microphone), *ammo* (ammunition).

Graphical abbreviations[33] mean that the word is formed from the initial letter of a word group, e. g.: *bf* (*boyfriend*). They may be further divided into two groups: letter abbreviations and acronyms.

1. **Letter abbreviations** are pronounced letter by letter: e. g.: *BBC [ˈbi:ˈbi:ˈsi:]* (the British Broadcasting Corporation), *EBRD [ˈi:ˈbi:ˈa:ˈdi:]* (European Bank for Reconstruction and Development), *M.P. [ˈemˈpi:]* (Member of Parliament), *M.S. [ˈemˈes]* (Master of Science), *M.C. [ˈemˈsi:]* (Master of Ceremonies, Member of Congress), *DJ [ˈdi:ˈd3ei]* (Disc Jockey) *CD [ˈsi:ˈdi:]* (compact disc), *CD-ROM* (Compact Disk Read Only Memory), *DVD [ˈdi:ˈvi:ˈdi:]* (digital video disk), *TV [ˈti:ˈvi:]* (television), *G.I. [ˈd3i:ˈai]* (Government Issue), *SOS [ˈesˈouˈes]* (Save Our Souls = 'urgent call for help'), *P.M. [ˈpi:ˈem]* (Prime Minister) *P.O.W.* (prisoner of war), *w.c.* (water closet), *P.G.* (paying guest), *B.C.* (before Christ), etc.;

---

32 Examples retrieved from https://studfile.net/preview/5650192/page:5/, accessed 12.03.2023.
33 Examples retrieved from https://studfile.net/preview/5650192/page:6/, accessed 12.03.2023.

2. **Acronyms** are vocabulary units pronounced as words. They may be divided
   into the following categories:
   - Acronyms formed from the initial letters of a phrase, e.g.:
     - **Formal acronyms,** e.g.: *UNO [juːnou]* (the United Nations Organ-
       isation), *NATO ['neitou]* (North Atlantic Treaty Organisation), *UNESCO
       [juːˈneskou]* (United Nations Educational, Scientific and Cultural Or-
       ganization); *AIDS, Aids ['eidz]* (Acquired Immuno-Deficiency Syn-
       drome), *maser ['meizə]* (microwave amplification by stimulated emis-
       sion of radiation), *laser ['leizə]* (light amplification by stimulated
       emission of radiation), *radar ['reidə]* (radio detection and ranging), etc.;
     - **Informal acronyms** *(SMS and chat abbreviations),* e.g.: *ASAP* (As Soon
       As Possible), *FAQ* (frequently asked questions), *FYI* (for your in-
       formation), *GIGO* (garbage in, garbage out), etc.;
   - Acronyms formed from the initial syllables of each word of the phrase, e.g.:
     Interpol (International police); *Incoterms* (International Commercial
     Terms), *tacsatcom* = Tactical Satellite Communications, etc.;
   - Acronyms formed by a combination of the abbreviation of the first
     member of the phrase with the last member undergoing no change at all,
     e.g.: *V-day* (Victory Day), *V-sign* (victory sign); *A-bomb* (atomic bomb), *H-
     bomb* (hydrogen bomb); *M-day* (mobilization day), *G-man* (Government
     man), *g-force* (gravity force), *e-mail* (electronic mail), *e-modem* (external
     modem), *F keys* (functional keys), *Z-hour* (zero-hour), *A Level* (Advanced
     Level); *O Level* (Ordinary Level); *m-commerce* (mobile commerce), *M-
     media* (multimedia) etc, *TV-set* (-program, -show, -canal, etc.), *H-bag*
     (handbag), *T-shirt,* etc.
3. **Latin abbreviations** are a specific type of abbreviations, sometimes they are
   read as Latin words and sometimes they are substituted by their English
   equivalents. Some examples are: *A.D.* (Lat *anno Domini*) – Common Era, after
   Christ, *a.i.* (Lat *ad interim*) – temporary, *ad lib* (Lat *ad libitum*) – at pleasure,
   a.m. ['ei'em] (Lat *ante meridiem*) – before noon, in the morning, *cf.* (Lat
   conferre) – compare, *etc.* (Lat *et cetera*) – and so on, *cp.* (Lat *comparare*) –
   compare, *e.g.* (Lat *exempli gratia*) – for example *ib.* (Lat *ibidem*) – in the same
   place, *id.* (Lat *idem*) – the same, *i.e.* (Lat *id est*) – that is, namely, *loc.cit.* (Lat
   locus citato) – in the passage cited, *ob.* (Lat *obiit*) – he (she) died, *q.v.* (Lat *quod
   vide*) – which see; *p.m.* (Lat *post meridiem*) – in the afternoon, *viz.* (Lat
   videlicet) – namely.

As regards note-taking for consecutive interpreting, the crucial aspect is that the
abbreviations used must be explicit and unambiguous for the interpreter who
needs to understand them immediately as, during the rendition process, there is
no time to think what a given abbreviation means. There is also one important

rule for the use of abbreviations in note-taking, i.e. they need to be, first and foremost, consistent, which means that if, for example, the interpreter has chosen the abbreviation *pop* to stand for *popular,* then he/she has to find other abbreviations to stand for other words starting with "pop-", for example to adopt *pop^{on}* for *population.* Also, another rule governing creating abbreviations states that the fewer strokes are written, the more time can be saved and therefore one may write the words the way they are heard, for instance: high- *hi;* know- *no;* free- *fre;* fee- *fe;* night- *nite;* etc. He/she may also drop the middle vowels as in: build- *bld;* legal- *lgl;* bulletin- *bltn;* save- *sv;* budget- *bjt;* etc. The interpreter may also write only the initial or the final vowels, for example: office- *ofs;* easy- *ez;* follow- *flo;* value- *vlu;* open- *opn;* etc. Sample words written down following this rule are listed in the table below. It should be noted that they are all recognizable even though the consonants are not doubled and some or all vowels are missing:

asmble	assemble
arpln	airplane
bmb	bomb
cmtee	committee
dgtl	digital
difrnce	difference
elfnt	elephant
hstry	history
ptrlum	petroleum
phlsphy	philosophy
zbr	zebra

Table 2: Sample abbreviations used in note-taking for consecutive interpreting (source: https://studfile.net/preview/5650192/page:6/, accessed 12.03.2023).

As regards the principles of creating abbreviations, Rozan (2002) proposes the following:
1. abbreviation of words – Rozan (2002, 16) suggests that if the word is longer than 4–5 letters, the interpreter should note it in an abbreviated form by writing down some of the first and last letters. For instance, whereas the abbreviation *Prod.* may stand for all of the following concepts: "production", "producer", "product" or "productivity", abbreviations Pr^{on}, Pr^{er}, Pr^{ct}, Pr^{vity} are unambiguous and will represent the mentioned concepts respectively;
2. abbreviations to indicate gender, number and tenses – to indicate gender or number, one may add ^{m} or ^{f}, or ^{n} to the symbol of the abbreviation (standing for: masculine, feminine and neuter gender respectively), whereas in order to indicate the tense, one may add $^{-ll}$ for the future and $^{-d}$ for the past tense;

3. abbreviating the register – this entails abbreviating expressions which are too long, by using a word which would convey the same meaning but, at the same time, would be significantly shorter, for instance: "In order to arrive at some conclusion" can be noted as "to end"; or "Taking into account the situation at the present time" can be noted as "as sit^on now"; "with the intention of/with the purpose of" can be noted as "to".

The following table offers a list of sample abbreviations (most of which have been formed according to the above-mentioned principles) to be applied when note-taking for consecutive interpreting:

1. kilometre	km	22. labour	lbr	43. especially	esp.
2. kilowatt	kw	23. people	pp	44. approximately	appr.
3. kilowatt hour	kwh	24. society	soc.	45. according	acc.
4. centimetre	cm	25. economy	eco.	46. abbreviation	abbr.
5. millimetre	mm	26. monetary	mon	47. example	eg
6. number	no	27. politics	pol	48. television	tv
7. figure	fig.	28. popular	pop	49. dictionary	dic
8. maximum	max	29. export	exp	50. computer	pc
9. minimum	mini	30. import	imp	51. technology	tech
10. hundred	h	31. professional	pro	52. electricity	elec
11. million	mil	32. production	prod	53. definition	def.
12. thousand	thou	33. department	dep	54. laboratory	lab
13. mathematic	math	34. bureau	bu.	55. recreation	rec
14. literature	lit.	35. agriculture	agr	56. university	uni.
15. chemistry	chem	36. industry	indus	57. individual	indiv
16. physics	phys	37. corporation	corp.	58. calculation	cal
17. hour	hr	38. company	com	59. problem	prob
18. Tuesday	Tue.	39. commerce	comm	60. influenza	flu
19. week	wk	40. information	info	61. system	sys
20. year	yr	41. tele-communication	telecom	62. president	pres
21. century	cen	42. limited	ltd	63. professor	prof.

Table 3: Sample abbreviations used in note-taking for consecutive interpreting (source: https://studfile.net/preview/5650192/page:6/, accessed 12.03.2023).

As for some common international organizations, their abbreviations should ideally be remembered by the interpreter. The contexts and settings in which of the interpreter works are varied, as are the possible topics that he/she may have to tackle during conferences and meetings, with the participation of people representing different international and/or local organizations, agencies and corporations, etc. The interpreter should have some background knowledge about those organizations. The table below lists some common names and their abbreviations:

Asian Development Bank	ADB
Asia-Pacific Economic Cooperation	APEC
Association of South-East Asia Nations	ASEAN
Economic Cooperation Organization	ECO
European Bank for Reconstruction and Development	EBRD
European Union	EU
Food and Agriculture Organization	FAO
International Atomic Energy Agency	IAEA
International Chamber of Commerce	ICC
International Criminal Police Organization	INTERPOL
International Federation of Consulting Engineers (Fédération Internationale Des Ingénieurs-Conseils)	FIDIC
International Monetary Fund	IMF
International Labour Organization	ILO
International Organization for Standardization	ISO
International Olympic Committee	IOC
North Atlantic Treaty Organization	NATO
Organization for Security and Cooperation in Europe	OSCE
Organization of Petroleum-Exporting Countries	OPEC
United Nations Children's Fund	UNICEF
United Nations Development Programme	UNDP
United Nations Educational, Scientific and Cultural Organization	UNESCO
United Nations High Commissioner for Refugees	UNHCR
World Bank	WB
World Health Organization	WHO
World Intellectual Property Organization	WIPO
World Trade Organization	WTO

Table 4: List of names of international organizations and agencies in abbreviations used in note-taking for consecutive interpreting (source: https://studfile.net/preview/5650192/page:6/, accessed 12.03.2023).

The nature of the notes taken will always be determined by the purpose of the speech to be interpreted. For instance, an informative speech typically requires full note-taking, paying particular attention to all the factual information. Similarly, a descriptive speech also needs full note-taking, but with an emphasis on aspects that accurately describe what is meant. An argumentative speech requires noting down less information but, what is significant here, are the connectors and keywords.[34]

Summing up this part of the chapter, one may say that note-taking may be considered a supporting technique, that has been and is constantly "[...] developed by practitioners for practitioners to help them retrieve part of their source text understanding from memory" (Kohn and Albl-Mikasa 2002, 257–258). The main idea behind note-taking is to reduce the processing effort while interpreting. Thus, the notes taken need to have the following features (Kohn and Albl-Mikasa 2002, 258):

- economy: notes should be as brief as possible;
- instantaneous seizability: the interpreter should be able to read the notes at a glance;
- individuality: note-taking is not governed by any obligatory rules or regulations.

Kohn and Albl-Mikasa (ibidem) also observe that "[...] anything that supports its function or that is subjectively felt to do so is admissible". This also includes the choice of the language in which notes are taken, which largely depends on the interpreter's individual preferences. Some claim that notes should be taken in the target language to help make a clear distinction between the two languages in the mind of the interpreter, as well as to reduce the risk of using a literal translation. However, some interpreters find it easier and faster to take notes in the source language and then use them to interpret the speech while automatically changing the language. There are also other professionals – and this is the case that will be discussed later on in this chapter – who take notes in both languages, using one in order to note down certain ideas, and the other for other concepts. Sometimes this decision is dictated by the fact that one of the corresponding words is shorter in one language and thus faster to note down. Therefore, every single interpreter should develop their own way that they would find the most convenient and reliable.

3.2   Using Symbols

According to Matyssek 1989 (after Kohn and Albl-Mikasa 2002, 258), note-taking signs should be as language-neutral as possible. This is because, as he claims, the interpreter needs to become detached from the source text surface structures and this can only be achieved with the help of a notation system that is independent of any of the languages involved. Also, a significant advantage is to develop such a

---

34 Ibidem.

notation system which would be applicable to all of the interpreter's working languages (for instance one proposed by Rozan 2002). Nevertheless, as Kohn and Albl-Mikasa (ibidem) observe, "[...] notation systems show clear evidence of source or target language influences – without detrimental effects on the interpreter's performance".

Kohn and Albl-Mikasa (2002, 259) define a notation system as "a notation language offering a surprisingly wide range of notation signs with lexical, syntactic and pragmatic values. Notation signs make deliberate use of natural languages and are shaped by various reduction, adaptation and iconization processes". These authors point out to the fact that a notation language is aimed at minimizing the interpreter's processing effort and, therefore, it should be designed to allow fast, economical and effective note-taking that is easy to master and is adapted to the preferences and strengths of the individual interpreter. Hence, notation languages frequently apply a variety of self-created or borrowed means of expression.

In his short video, Andy Gillies (2017)[35] offers valuable advice to interpreters and interpreting trainees on how to use symbols for note-taking. First of all, he states that in order for symbols to be effective, one needs to use them as part of a structured and consistent note-taking system. Symbols offer considerable advantages as they are quick and easy to write, as well as quicker than words to read back. Another significant benefit behind symbols is that they represent concepts rather than words, which offers the interpreter a lot of freedom and flexibility as to which word to use in order to express a particular concept. Additionally, symbols save space on the page, as they take up less of it than words, which, in turn, facilitates introducing a clear structure to the notes.

As to what to replace with symbols, Gillies (ibidem) suggests the following:
- words that are repeated multiple times throughout the speech (e. g. words like *think, say, know, want, policy, industry, problem*; expressions like *I'm happy to*; *thank you,* etc.);
- words and expressions that are going to be used a lot during a particular speech, depending on its subject (e. g. if the subject is telecommunications, one may draw a simple picture of an antenna and use it throughout the meeting as a symbol to signify "telecommunications").

An extremely important aspect that Gillies mentions is that any symbol that is used needs to be clear and unambiguous. For instance, although all of the symbols presented below are based on the letters "e/a", they are clearly different from each other and thus unlikely to be confused.

---

35 https://www.lourdesderioja.com/2017/01/25/symbols-dos-and-donts/, accessed 1.03.2023.

€ Euro
E energy
e the economy
@ the environment

Symbols also have to be consistent, so for instance if **E** is selected as a symbol for "energy", it would always have to be used with this meaning only. Also, any symbol chosen has to be meaningful to the person who selected it. It is therefore inadvisable to try to adopt symbols used by someone else. Symbols might be drawn for instance from mathematics, science, music, etc., but if they do not really "click" with the person who is going to use them, then they will not be effective or reliable in the long run.

Symbols should also be organic, i.e. one symbol may serve as a root from which one may build other related symbols, for example the symbol of an arrow:

↗ to rise
↘ to fall
↓ going down to zero ("destruction", "elimination", etc.)
← going backwards ("to come from somewhere", "to derive from", etc.)

Another example of such an organic symbol might be the symbol "x" used to mean "time", on the basis of which the following variations are possible:

x–	timeless, eternal
xx	many times, often
xx+	many times more
xx–	many times less
x t x	from time to time, occasionally
=x	equal time
+x	more time, longer time
–x	less time, shorter time
2x	twice
3x-/	three times less than
100x	a hundred times
100x+	a hundred times more
Ltdx	a limited time
oldx	old-time, old fashioned
x!	It's time, the time has come
gdx	a good time
x)	time limit, deadline
x>	future

<x	past
ovrx	overtime
xng	timing
xtbl	timetable, schedule
prtx	part-time
x,x	time after time, repeatedly
wrx	wartime

Table 5: Variations of the symbol "x" indicating "time" (source: https://studfile.net/previe w/5650192/page:7/, accessed 13.03.2023).

James Nolan in his book *Interpretation. Techniques and Exercises* offers some basic guidelines on using symbols and abbreviations for note-taking (Nolan 2012, 295):
– one should adopt symbols that would be useful for the subject matters of the meetings and conferences one will be interpreting at;
– a symbol needs to have only one meaning in a given context;
– simple pictures and drawings such as circles, squares, lines and arrows, may be used;
– notes should be arranged on the page in a meaningful way (for instance, the main points at the top, followed by those of lesser importance);
– conventional abbreviations and acronyms should be used (such as ones illustrated in the previous subchapter);
– a one-stroke symbol may be adopted to mean "the main subject of the speech";
– a simple sign can be adopted to mean "three zeroes", so that one will be able to write down large numbers quickly (for example, if "–" means "three zeroes", then "89 – –" means "89 million"); another symbol may be adopted to represent two zeroes;
– symbols for certain prefixes and suffixes may be coined, such as "pre-", "anti-", "-ion", "-ment".
– when writing down words, one may not double the consonants and delete any vowels that are not necessary to make the word recognizable.

Obviously, one may use the already existing symbols derived from different scientific or artistic disciplines, as well as areas of everyday life:

Maths	= + > < % /
Science	E μ t ^oC
Music	# ♪ ♫ ♫
Text messages	L8R R U OK? HRU? ASAP 2
Keyboard	% & @ ¶ ™
Punctuation marks	? ! ( ) " :

Vehicle registrations	D DA UK CH F
Short words in other languages	So hi ta ok / bo ale juz / deja / ergo etc / pero
Currencies	$ Y L € £
Periodic table	Fe Na Po Mg Ag CO_2 CO NO_2 H_2SO_4

Table 6. Sample symbols used in note-taking for consecutive interpreting (source: https://studfile.net/preview/5650192/page:14/, accessed 12.03.2023).

Other possible sources of symbols might be:[36]
- symbols or abbreviations from dictionary entries, like ~ ;
- some common business and commercial symbols and abbreviations, like @, £, CIF or ASAP;
- letters from foreign alphabets;
- pictographs borrowed from languages such as Chinese (for example β to mean "standing");
- punctuation marks like ! or ? or / (for example, one may use +/ to mean "and or", and the ampersand (&) to mean "and");
- signs of the zodiac;
- pronunciation symbols, accents, diacritical marks;
- capital letters used for a specific meaning, like "P" to mean president, or "F" to mean France; or single letters used for a specific meaning, like "c" to mean "country";
- children's "picture-writing" (e.g. ∧ to mean "house" or "shelter", or ☺ to mean "happy" or "pleased", or ♥ to mean "love");
- scientific symbols, like ♂ for "a man", and ♀ for "a woman";
- musical signs;
- legal symbols, like § to mean "section";
- monograms (combinations of letters, such as Æ).

Below are some sample symbols designed by a practising interpreter, Paula López (2021),[37] which may serve as an inspiration for creating one's own:

according to	agriculture	all every	usiness	but	buy

36 Examples retrieved from https://studfile.net/preview/5650192/page:7/, accessed 13.03.2023.
37 https://paulainterprete.com/en/list-of-symbols-for-consecutive-interpretation/, accessed 12.03.2023.

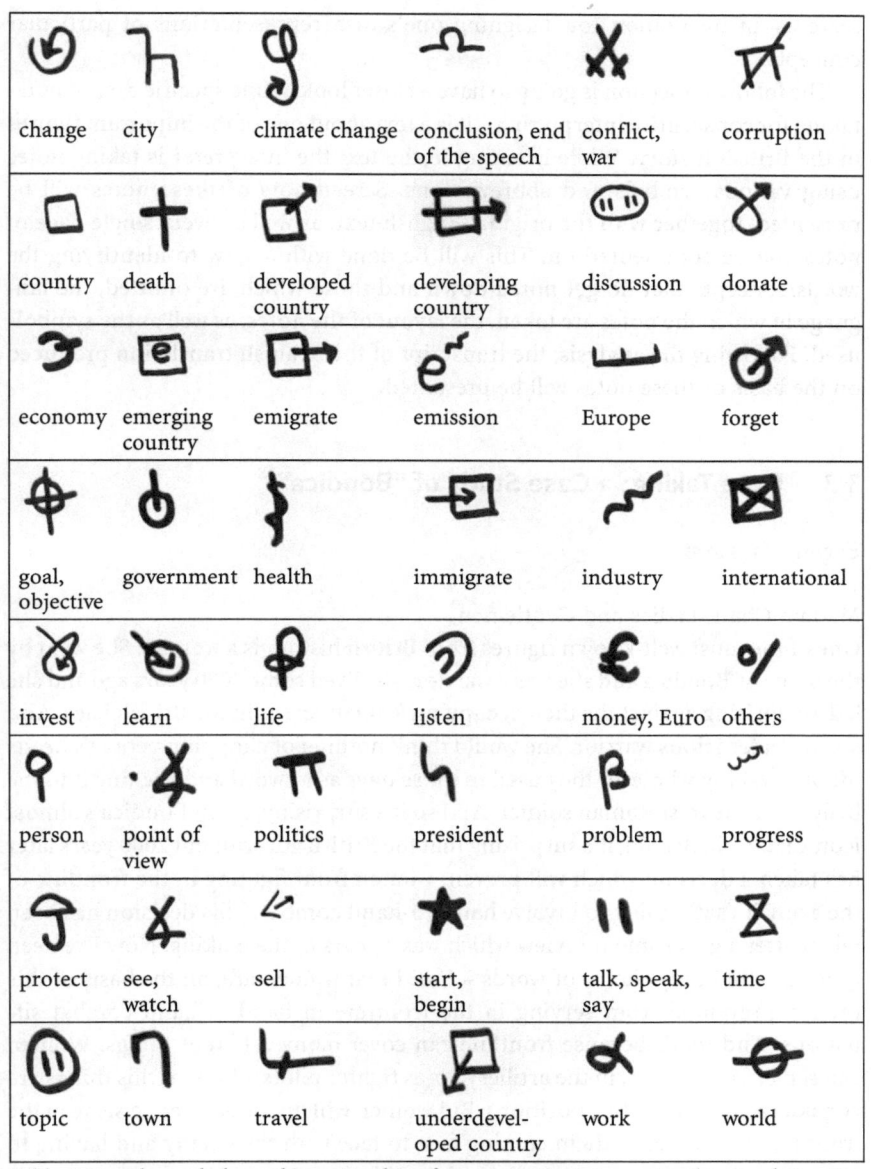

change	city	climate change	conclusion, end of the speech	conflict, war	corruption
country	death	developed country	developing country	discussion	donate
economy	emerging country	emigrate	emission	Europe	forget
goal, objective	government	health	immigrate	industry	international
invest	learn	life	listen	money, Euro	others
person	point of view	politics	president	problem	progress
protect	see, watch	sell	start, begin	talk, speak, say	time
topic	town	travel	underdeveloped country	work	world

Table 7. Sample symbols used in note-taking for consecutive interpreting (source: https://paulainterprete.com/en/list-of-symbols-for-consecutive-interpretation/, accessed 12.03. 2023).

If one is running out of ideas of what kind of symbols to create for certain concepts, the website http://www.symbolovnik.cz/en can be of excellent help and serve as an inspiration for designing one's own representations of particular concepts.

The following section is going to have a closer look at one specific case of note-taking for consecutive interpreting – it is a text about one of the important figures in the British history. While listening to the text the interpreter is taking notes using various symbols and abbreviations. Screenshots of these notes will be presented, together with the original English text, as well as every single page of notes will be commented on. This will be done with a view to identifying the words/concepts that do get noted down and those which are omitted, the language in which the notes are taken, the layout of the notes, as well as the symbols used. Following the analysis, the transcript of the Spanish translation produced on the basis of these notes will be presented.

3.3   Note Taking: a Case Study of "Boudica"[38]

English transcript

Madam Chair, Ladies and Gentlemen,
One of the most well-known figures from British history is a woman. She went by the name of Boudica and she was a warrior. She lived some 2000 years ago and she led an uprising against the then occupying Roman forces in the British Isles. And she was a ferocious warrior. She would think nothing of chopping people's heads off or of taking whatever they used in those days as a sword and sticking it to the belly of the nearest Roman soldier. And so it's surprising, given Boudica's almost iconic status in Britain, it's surprising that the British government 2000 years later has taken a decision which will prevent women from fighting in the frontline of the army if that's going to involve hand-to-hand combat. This decision has been taken after a government review which was 4 years in the making. Now I've been quite careful in my choice of words – I said that women are, on the basis of this review, prevented from serving in the frontline in hand-to-hand combat situations. And that's because frontline can cover many different things. Women can serve, for example, in the artillery, or as fighter pilots – both of this things are considered to be frontline positions. But women will not be allowed to serve in the frontline if that means them coming face to face with the enemy and having to engage in physical hand-to-hand combat with the enemy.

---

38 Here I would like to express my sincere gratitude to Lourdes de Rioja for granting me her permission to use the screenshots from the video entitled: "A consecutive demo: Boudica" (link: https://www.youtube.com/watch?v=Cz3fjAX5Meg&t=54s).

As a result of this decision, some 30% of all the jobs open in the army are unavailable to women, women can't take up those posts. So why has the government taken this decision? There are a number of reasons.

Firstly, the government argues that modern warfare is intensely physical and women simply don't have the strength that is required in order to do the job. To give you an example, you may have a situation in which a soldier is wounded. Your responsibility is to pick up that soldier – and we're talking: big guys, guys that can weigh 80 kg, even 90 kg – you have to pick him up and carry him back to safety behind your own life. You also have to carry your own equipment – 15 kg – and his equipment – another 15 kg. Now that's an awful lot of weight to have to carry around, and the government says that women simply don't have the strength, particularly the upper body strength, to be able to do that.

Now, the second reason that the government doesn't want women in hand-to-hand combat situation has to do more with the nature of the modern warfare. Modern warfare is largely mechanized, by which I mean it's fought using tanks and armoured cars. Now, your average tank crew – 6–7 men – will have to spend a very long time in the confined, cramped, sweaty space that is the inside of a tank, and they may have to be there for 24, maybe even 36 hours at a stretch, during which time there is only one possibility of relieving themselves: there is a chemical toilet which is placed underneath the driver's seat. The argument goes that it's already rather embarrassing for a man to have to use this chemical toilet, surrounded by his colleagues, it would be even more embarrassing for a women to have to do so.

And the third argument that the government gives has to do with the fact that allowing women to serve in hand-to-hand combat situations is basically an experiment. You don't known whether a woman is going to be able to hack it in such a situation until you actually try it out. But what happens if you have a woman in the frontline and she finds herself faced with a 2-meter tall animal of a man running at her with his bayonet pointed directly at her belly. She suddenly decides: "actually, this isn't such a good idea, maybe I could change my mind?" But of course she can't. And a s a result of this uncertainty perhaps, people – say the government – are likely to die. There's simply not worth putting people's lives at risk in order to prove that you have a pro-women, politically correct policy in place – say the government.

So that's the policy of the British government. Now, other countries are somewhat more enlightened than we are. In Denmark and Norway, for example, women are allowed to serve in all positions of the army, including frontline, hand-to-hand combat positions. That's perhaps understandable given that these Scandinavian countries have a long-standing tradition of gender equality, of treating men and women absolutely equally.

But we shouldn't get carried away because the fact is that although women could serve in hand-to-hand situations, in fact none do in any of these countries. The reason given by military authorities in Norway and Denmark is quite simply that no woman has yet fulfilled the job conditions. Obviously, they haven't met Margaret Thatcher yet. And also it's interesting to see that in fact this more enlightened open policy doesn't encourage more women into the army. Women make up about 8% of the personnel in the army and the navy in the United Kingdom. In the United States which has exactly the same policy as the United Kingdom, women make up as many as 16% of the armed forces.

Compare that to the situation in Denmark and Norway. Women make up 5% of the army in Denmark and only 3% in Norway.

So, what's my conclusion? Well, basically, it's this: if you're a woman and you feel that it's your inalienable right as a woman to serve in the army in exactly the same way as a man might, then I suggest that there are two courses of action open to you:

1. If you want to avail yourself of your right to go to the toilet surrounded by 6 or 7 battle-hardened and probably sex-starved men, or if you want to avail yourself of your right to have somebody charge at you with a bayonet, screaming as they do so – then fine, go ahead and marry a Norwegian or a Dane
2. If, however, you think it might be a little bit more fun to fly a stealth bomber – well, in that case perhaps you could consider marrying an American instead.

Thank you very much for your attention.

Polish translation

Pani Przewodnicząca, Panie i Panowie,
Jedną z najbardziej znanych postaci w historii Wielkiej Brytanii jest kobieta. Miała na imię Boudika i była wojowniczką. Żyła około 2000 lat temu i poprowadziła powstanie przeciwko ówczesnym okupantom rzymskim na Wyspach Brytyjskich. Była zaciekłą wojowniczką. Nie miała skrupułów, żeby odrąbywać ludziom głowy albo chwycić za coś, co w tamtych czasach używano w charakterze miecza, i wbić to w brzuch najbliższego rzymskiego żołnierza. Zaskakujące jest więc, biorąc pod uwagę niemal kultowy status Boudiki w Wielkiej Brytanii, że rząd brytyjski 2000 lat później podjął decyzję, która uniemożliwiła kobietom walkę na linii frontu, jeśli miałaby ona wiązać się z walką wręcz. Decyzja ta została podjęta po analizie przeprowadzonej przez komisję rządową, która trwała 4 lata. Chcąc ostrożnie dobrać słowa, powiem, że na podstawie tej analizy zdecydowano, że kobiety nie mogą służyć na linii frontu w sytuacjach walki wręcz. Linia frontu może obejmować wiele różnych sytuacji. Kobiety mogą

służyć na przykład w artylerii lub jako piloci myśliwców – obie te pozycje zaliczane są do frontowych. Ale kobiety nie mogą służyć na linii frontu, jeśli oznacza to, że staną twarzą w twarz z przeciwnikiem i będą musiały angażować się w fizyczną walkę wręcz z wrogiem.

W wyniku tej decyzji około 30% wszystkich wolnych wakatów w wojsku jest niedostępnych dla kobiet, kobiety nie mogą zajmować tych stanowisk. Dlaczego więc rząd podjął taką decyzję? Istnieje wiele powodów.

Po pierwsze, rząd argumentuje, że współczesny sposób prowadzenia wojny ma bardzo fizyczny charakter, a kobiety po prostu nie mają siły potrzebnej do wykonywania tej pracy. Przykładowo może dojść do sytuacji, w której żołnierz jest ranny. Twoim obowiązkiem jest podniesienie tego żołnierza – a mówimy o mężczyźnie sporych rozmiarów, który może ważyć 80 czy nawet 90 kg – musisz go podnieść i przenieść w bezpieczne miejsce, narażając własne życie. Musisz przy tym też przenieść własny sprzęt – 15 kg – i jego sprzęt – kolejne 15 kg. Jest to naprawdę spory ciężar do udźwignięcia, dlatego rząd twierdzi, że kobiety po prostu nie mają wystarczająco siły, szczególnie w górnych partiach ciała, aby być w stanie to zrobić.

Drugi powód, dla którego rząd nie pozwala kobietom angażować się w walkę wręcz jest związany z naturą współczesnej wojny. Współczesne starcia militarne są w dużej mierze zmechanizowane i odbywają się przy użyciu czołgów i samochodów opancerzonych. Przeciętna załoga czołgu – 6–7 osób – będzie musiała spędzić bardzo dużo czasu w ograniczonej, ciasnej, przepoconej przestrzeni, jaką jest wnętrze czołgu, i musi tam przebywać przez 24, a może nawet 36 godzin, w którym to czasie istnieje tylko jedna możliwość załatwienia swoich potrzeb fizjologicznych: pod siedzeniem kierowcy znajduje się toaleta chemiczna. Już dla mężczyzny korzystanie z toalety chemicznej w otoczeniu kolegów jest wystarczająco krępujące, a co dopiero dla kobiety.

Trzeci argument, który podaje rząd, dotyczy faktu, że pozwolenie kobietom na służbę na linii frontu byłoby w zasadzie eksperymentem. Po prostu nie wiadomo, czy kobieta byłaby w stanie sobie z tym poradzić. Co by się stało w sytuacji, gdy na kobietę znajdującą się na linii frontu biegnie nagle 2-metrowy mężczyzna z bagnetem skierowanym w jej brzuch. Może ona wtedy dojść do wniosku: "Właściwie to nie jest taki dobry pomysł, może mogłabym zmienić zdanie"? Ale oczywiście już teraz nie może. Rząd argumentuje więc, że w takiej sytuacji śmierć mogłoby ponieść wiele kobiet, w związku z czym nie chce narażać ich życia tylko po to, by udowodnić, że prowadzi politykę równouprawnienia.

Takie jest stanowisko rządu brytyjskiego. Inne kraje są jednak nieco bardziej postępowe w tej kwestii. Na przykład w Danii i Norwegii kobiety mogą służyć na wszystkich stanowiskach w armii, w tym na linii frontu w sytuacjach walki wręcz. Jest to być może zrozumiałe, biorąc pod uwagę, że te kraje skandynawskie mają długą tradycję prowadzenia polityki równości płci, traktowania mężczyzn i kobiet absolutnie jednakowo.

Ale nie powinniśmy dać się ponieść emocjom, ponieważ faktem jest, że chociaż kobiety mogą służyć w sytuacjach walki wręcz, w rzeczywistości żadna z nich tego nie robi. Powodem, jak podają władze w Norwegii i Danii, jest to, że żadna kobieta nie spełniła jeszcze warunków potrzebnych do uzyskania takiego stanowiska. Najwyraźniej nie spotkali jeszcze Margaret Thatcher. Ciekawe jest również to, że w rzeczywistości ta bardziej postępowa, otwarta polityka nie zachęca większej liczby kobiet do zatrudnienia się w wojsku. Kobiety stanowią około 8% personelu armii i marynarki wojennej Wielkiej Brytanii. W Stanach Zjednoczonych, które prowadzą w tej kwestii dokładnie taką samą politykę jak Wielka Brytania, kobiety stanowią aż 16% sił zbrojnych.

Porównajmy to z sytuacją w Danii i Norwegii. Kobiety stanowią 5% personelu armii w Danii i tylko 3% w Norwegii.

Jaki jest wniosek? Cóż, w zasadzie wygląda to tak: jeśli jesteś kobietą i czujesz, że twoim niezbywalnym prawem jako kobiety jest służba w wojsku na dokładnie takich samych prawach, jak mężczyzna, to masz do wyboru jedną z dwóch opcji:

1. Jeśli chcesz skorzystać z prawa do pójścia do toalety w otoczeniu 6 lub 7 zaprawionych w bojach i prawdopodobnie napalonych seksualnie mężczyzn, lub jeśli chcesz skorzystać z prawa do tego, by ktoś zaatakował cię bagnetem, krzycząc przy tym niemiłosiernie – to dobrze, śmiało wyjdź za mąż za Norwega lub Duńczyka.

2. Jeśli jednak uważasz, że wolałabyś polatać sobie bombowcem stealth – cóż, w takim razie możesz rozważyć poślubienie Amerykanina.

Dziękuję bardzo za uwagę.

Analysis

English original
Madam **Chair, Ladies** and **Gentlemen,** one of the most **well-known figures** from **British history** is a **woman.** She went by the name of **Boudica** and she was a **warrior.** She lived some **2000 years ago**

Screenshot 1[39]

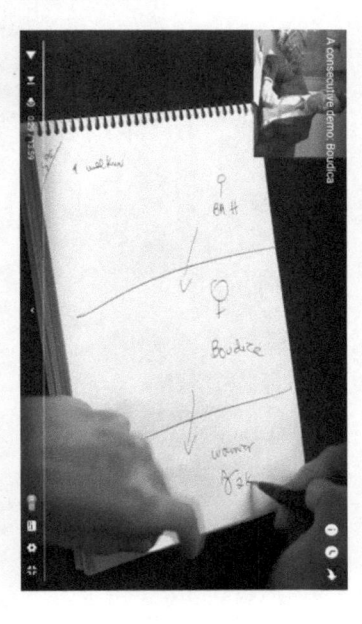

Comments
In the left-hand corner there are letters "LG" meaning "ladies and gentlemen", as well as a symbol of chair, which appears to be a very creative way of indicating the concept of "Madam Chair". What also gets noted down is the number "1", the word "well-known", the symbol of a person, as well as the letters "BR H" standing for "British history". Below is a symbol of the female gender used in biology, together with the name "Boudica". Underneath follows the word "warrior" and the number "2k" (meaning 2000) with an arrow pointing to the left (indicating the concept of "ago").

---

39 All images used in this section of the book courtesy of Lourdes de Rioja.

English original

and she led an **uprising against** the then occupying **Roman** forces in the **British Isles.** And she was a ferocious warrior. She would think nothing of **chopping people's heads off** or of taking whatever they used in those days as a **sword** and **sticking it** to the **belly** of the nearest **Roman soldier.** And so it's **surprising,** given **Boudica's** almost iconic status in Britain

Screenshot 2

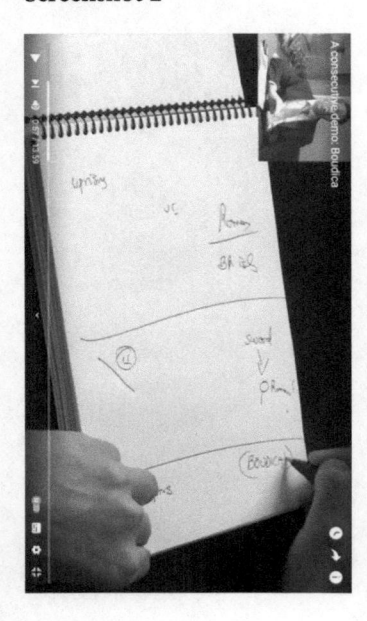

Comments

On top of the page there is the word "uprising", "vs" (meaning "against"), "Romans" and immediately below "BR Isles". The next sentence is separated from the previous one by a horizontal line stretching throughout the entire page. The idea of "chopping people's heads off" is expressed by a picture of a sad-looking face and a diagonal line indicating the concept of "cutting". Then there is the word "sword" and an arrow indicates the place where the sword is being stuck, i. e. into a Roman soldier (here again the symbol of a person is used). In the following sentence there is "surprs" meaning "surprising" and again the name "Boudica" is repeated, this time in the genitive form and in round brackets indicating an additional remark.

English original

that the **British government 2000 years later** has taken a **decision** which will **prevent women from fighting** in the frontline of the army **if** that's going to involve **hand-to-hand combat.** This **decision** has been taken **after a government review** which was **4 years** in the making.

Screenshot 3

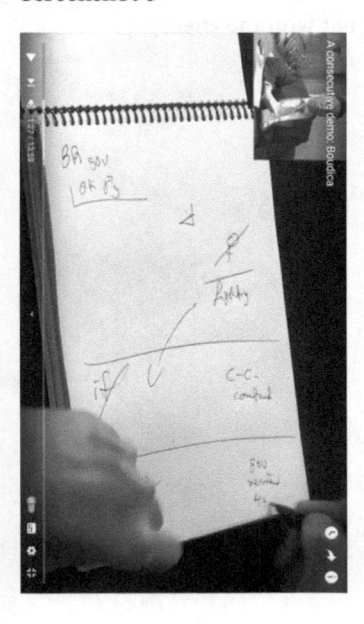

Comments

The notes for this sentence are continued on the next page. The interpreter uses the abbreviation "BR gov" standing for the "British government", "2k" and an arrow pointing to the right together with the letter "y" indicating the concept of "2000 years later". What follows in the middle of this section of the page is a symbol for "decision". Then there is a crossed out symbol of the female gender and the word "fighting" immediately underneath, all of which together express the idea of "preventing women from fighting". The connector "if" also gets noted down, together with "C-C- confront.", where "C-C" stands for "cuerpo a cuerpo" which in Spanish means "hand-to-hand". Below, on the left-hand side of the page there is a symbol of decision, together with the word "after", and on the right-hand side there is "gov review" and "4y", meaning "4 years".

English original
Now I've been quite **careful in my choice of words** – I said that **women** are, on the basis of this review, prevented from serving in the frontline in **hand-to-hand combat situations.** And that's because **frontline** can cover many different things. **Women** can serve, for example, in the **artillery**, or as fighter **pilots** – both of this things are considered to be **frontline** positions. **But women** will not be allowed to serve in the frontline if that means them coming face to face with the enemy and having to engage in physical **hand-to-hand combat** with the **enemy.**

Screenshot 4

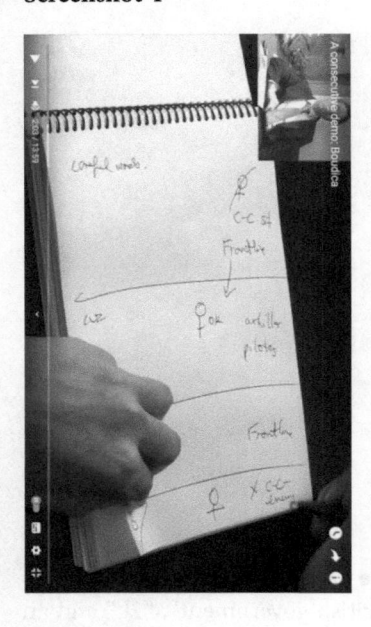

Comments
On this screenshot, first of all, we can see the words "careful vocab." which corresponds with the phrase "careful with my choice of words". Then there is the female gender symbol that is crossed out, immediately underneath there is "C-C sit." standing for "hand-to-hand combat situations", as well as the word "frontline" placed just below. In the following sentence the interpreter notes down the linking word "cuz" meaning "because" and repeated the female gender symbol followed with "OK" plus two words: "artillery" and "pilots", both of which are considered to be frontline positions, hence the word "frontline" underneath. What follows is the letter "B" standing for the conjunction "but", and again the symbol of a woman plus the already used "C-C-" and the word "enemy".

English original
As a **result** of this decision, some **30%** of all the **jobs** open in the **army** are **unavailable** to **women,** women can't take up those posts. So **why** has the **government** taken this **decision?** There are a number of **reasons.**

Screenshot 5

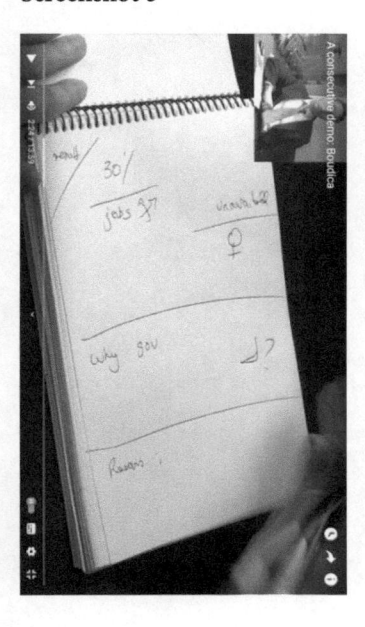

Comments
In the left-hand corner of the page we can see the word "result" and the number "30%", as well as the word "jobs" and a symbol of two crossed arrows indicating the concept of "the army". What follows is the word "unavailable" and the symbol of the female gender just below the word. In the next sentence the interpreter noted down the question word "why", the abbreviation "gov." and again the symbol for a "decision". Below there is the word "reasons" followed by a semicolon indicating that what is going to follow will be an enumeration.

English original

Firstly, the government argues that **modern warfare** is intensely **physical** and **women** simply **don't have the strength** that is required in order to do the job. To give you an **example,** you may have a situation in which **a soldier is wounded. Your** responsibility is to **pick up** that soldier –

Screenshot 6

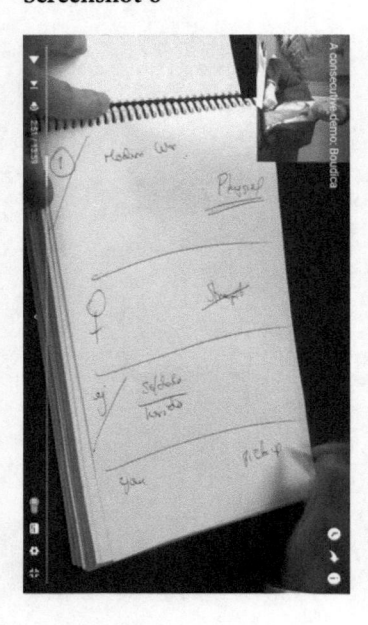

Comments

Number "1" indicates the first reason, the expression "modern war." and the word "physical" underlined twice mean that "modern warfare is intensely physical" (the double underlining of the word "physical" strengthens the meaning of the word). What follows is the symbol of a woman and the word "strength" which has been crossed out. The abbreviation "ej" means "ejemplo" in Spanish ("example" in English), and the example concerns "soldado herido", i. e. "a wounded soldier". Then the interpreter noted down the pronoun "you" and the phrasal verb "pick up".

English original

and we're talking: big guys, guys that can weigh **80 kg**, even **90 kg** – you have to pick him up and carry him back **to safety** behind your own life. **You** also **have to carry** your own **equipment** – **15 kg** – and his equipment – another **15 kg**. Now that's **an awful lot of weight** to have to carry around

Screenshot 7

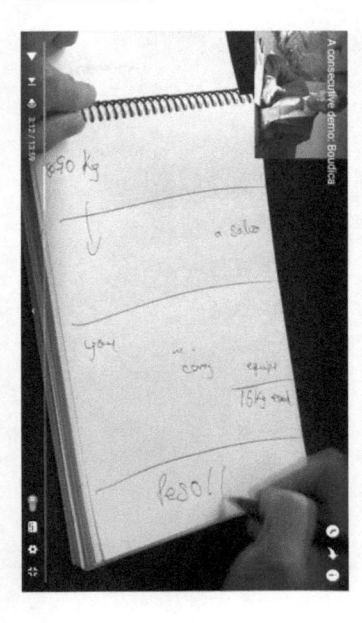

Comments

Here, the sentence is continued, so the interpreter notes down the weight of the potential soldier ("80–90 kg"), and then writes down "a salvo" which is a Spanish phrase meaning "to safety". Then the pronoun "you" is repeated, followed with the letter "m." meaning "must", as well as the word "carry" followed with the Spanish word "equipo" (meaning "equipment") underlined with one line and immediately below "15 kg" and "anot" standing for "another" (meaning "the equipment of another soldier"). Underneath the word "peso" (meaning "weight") with two exclamation marks indicates the concept expressed by the expression "an awful lot of weight".

English original

and the **government** says that women simply **don't have the strength, particularly the upper body strength,** to be able to do that.

Now, **the second reason** that the government doesn't want women in hand-to-hand combat situation has to do more with the **nature of the modern warfare.** Modern warfare is largely **mechanized,** by which I mean it's fought using **tanks** and armoured cars.

Screenshot 8

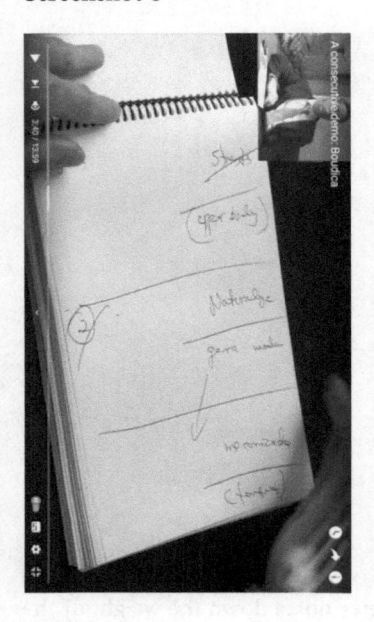

Comments

In the left-hand corner there is the abbreviation "gov." standing for "the government". What follows is the word "strength" which has been crossed out, and immediately underneath – the expression "upper body" in round brackets indicating an example or a comment which adds more precision to the statement. In the next sentence there is the number "2" meaning "the second reason", and then "naturaleza" (meaning: "nature") and "guerra moderna" ("modern warfare"). The arrow indicates an immediate connection between "modern warfare" and "mechanizada" ("mechanized"). The word "tanques" (meaning "tanks") included in round brackets, which is added immediately under the word "mechanizada", indicates an example.

English original

Now, your average **tank crew – 6–7 men** – will have to spend a very long time in the confined, cramped, sweaty space that is the **inside of a tank**, and they may have to be there for **24**, maybe even **36 hours at a stretch**, during which time there is only **one possibility** of relieving themselves: there is a **chemical toilet** which is placed **underneath the** driver's **seat**

Screenshot 9

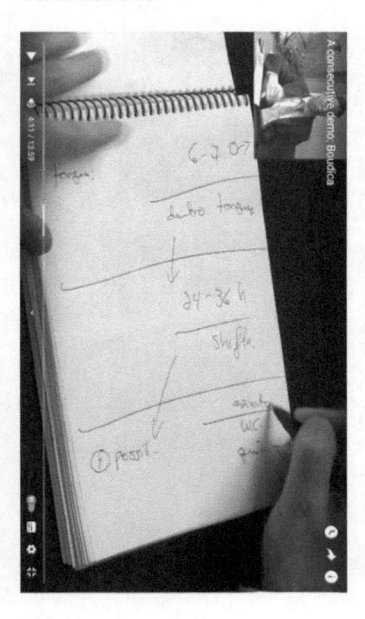

Comments

Here the interpreter noted down the word "tanque:" followed with the numbers "6–7" and the symbol of the male gender. Immediately underneath follows the expression "dentro tanque" (meaning "inside the tank"). Below we can see "24–36 h" indicating the time those men are spending in the tank, the interpreter also wrote down the word "shifts" which, although not mentioned in the original text, successfully conveys the nature of those men's job. Then there is the expression "1 possib." indicating "the only possibility" and then the word "asiento" (meaning: "a seat") and the phrase "W.C. químico" immediately underneath are positioned in a way that successfully illustrates the location of the chemical toilet mentioned (i.e. "underneath the seat").

English original

The **argument** goes that it's already rather **embarrassing** for a **man** to have to use this chemical toilet, surrounded by his colleagues, it would be **even more embarrassing for a women** to have to do so.

And **the third argument** that the government gives has to do with the fact that allowing women to **serve in hand-to-hand combat situations** is basically an **experiment.**

Screenshot 10

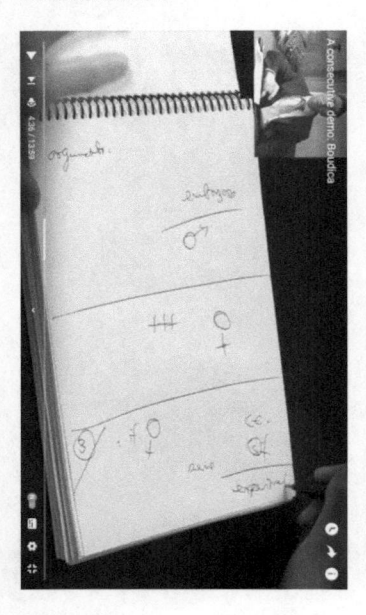

Comments

The interpreter noted down the word "argument" and then "embarazoso" (meaning: "embarrassing") followed by the symbol of the male gender. Below, the three pluses and the symbol of the female gender convey the idea of "it's even more embarrassing for a woman". In the next sentence the interpreter noted down the number "3" indicating the third argument, the connector "if" followed by the symbol of the female gender, the word "serve" and again the symbol "C-C-sit." (meaning "hand-to-hand combat situations"), as well as the word "experiment" immediately underneath.

English original

You **don't know** whether a woman is going to be able to hack it in such a situation **until** you actually **try it out.** But **what** happens if you have a woman in the frontline and she finds herself faced with a 2-meter tall **animal of a man running at her with his bayonet pointed directly at her belly.** She suddenly decides: "actually, this isn't such a good **idea,** maybe I could **change my mind?"** But of course she can't.

Screenshot 11

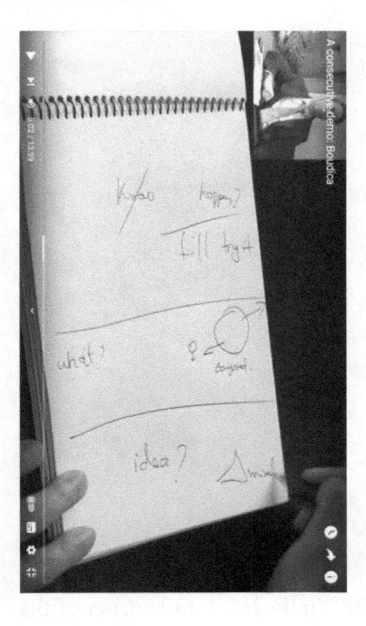

Comments

The word "know" which has been crossed out, followed by "happen" with the question mark, and "till try it" immediately below, all express the concept "you don't know what will happen until you try it out". In the next sentence the interpreter indicated a question by noting down the word "what" with a question mark. Then the interpreter drew a small symbol of the female gender and a significantly bigger symbol of the male gender together with an arrow (here illustrating a "bayonet") pointing at the symbol of the female gender. There is also the word "bayonet" noted down by the interpreter in order not to confuse the arrow with any other concept it could potentially stand for. Below we can see the word "idea" followed with a question mark, the triangle which symbolizes a change, and the word "mind".

English original
And a s a **result** of this uncertainty perhaps, **people** – say the government – **are likely to die.** There's simply **not worth** putting people's lives at **risk** in order to prove that you have a **pro-women**, politically correct **policy** in place – say the government.

Screenshot 12

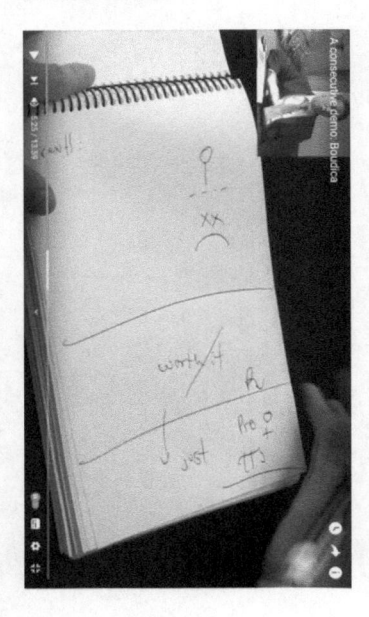

Comments
Here, the interpreter noted down the word "result:" in the left-hand corner of the page and followed it with a symbol of a person, and then a dead face immediately underneath having crosses in place of eyes. Below we can see the expression "worth it" crossed out, which indicates a negation (the idea of "it's not worth it"), the capital letter "R" meaning "risk" and then the linking word "just" followed by the abbreviation "pro" and the symbol of the female gender, as well as the symbol of "policy" immediately underneath (which looks just like the symbol of the number pi Π).

English original

So that's the policy of the British government. Now, **other countries** are somewhat more **enlightened than we are.** In **Denmark** and **Norway**, for example, **women** are **allowed** to serve in **all positions** of the army, including frontline, **hand-to-hand** combat positions. That's perhaps **understandable given that** these Scandinavian countries have a long-standing **tradition** of **gender equality,**

Screenshot 13

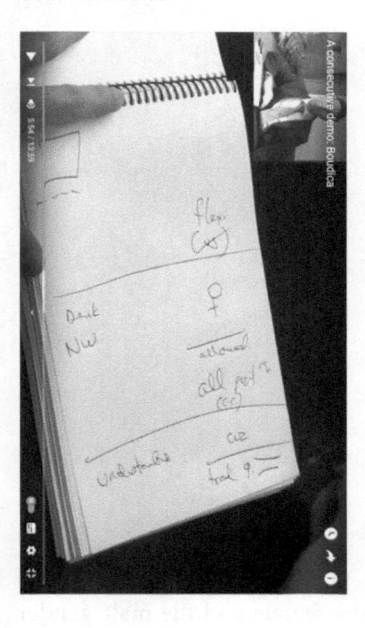

Comments

The big square in the left-hand corner of the page underlined with a dotted line signifies "other countries". The abbreviation "flexi" stands for the concept of being "flexible" which corresponds to the original "more enlightened". This is closely connected with the word "us" which has been placed in round brackets and crossed out. In the following sentence the interpreter noted down two abbreviations of countries "Denk" and "Nw" meaning Denmark and Norway respectively. What follows is the symbol of the female gender underlined with a straight horizontal line and the word "allowed" coming immediately under "all posit.^{ns}" and "C-C.", meaning "women are allowed to serve in all positions, including hand-to-hand combat". In the next sentence the interpreter noted down the word "understandable" and then the conjunction "cuz" standing for "because", again underlined with a straight horizontal line, below which she noted "trad. g =", meaning "tradition of gender equality".

English original
of treating **men and women** absolutely equally. But we **shouldn't get carried away because** the fact is that although **women could** serve in hand-to-hand situations, in fact **none do** in any of these countries.

Screenshot 14

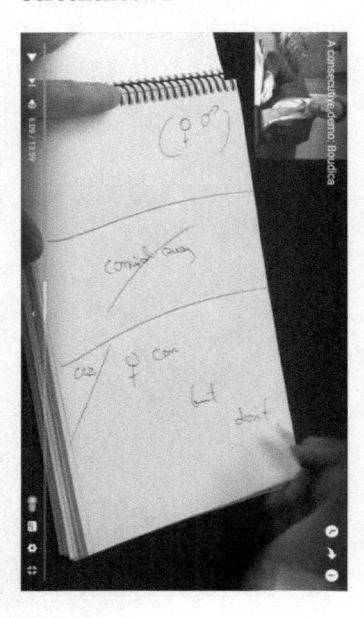

Comments
The first symbols visible on this page, that is the female and the male gender symbols placed in round brackets are the continuation of the previous sentence, i. e. expressing the idea of "treating men and women equally". What follows is the expression "carried away" which has been crossed out indicating the negation. Then the interpreter noted down the conjunction "because" in its shortened form "cuz", followed by the symbol of the female gender and then the modal verb "can", as well as the conjunction "but" immediately below and the contraction "don't" even lower, all of which convey the idea that "women could serve in hand-to-hand situations but in fact none do".

English original

The **reason** given by military authorities in Norway and Denmark is quite simply that **no woman has yet fulfilled the job conditions.** Obviously, they **haven't met** Margaret **Thatcher** yet. And also it's interesting to see that in fact this more enlightened open **policy doesn't encourage more women into the army.**

Screenshot 15

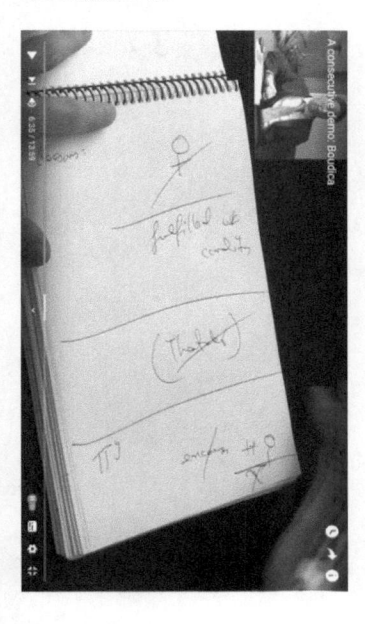

Comments

Here, the first word noted by the interpreter is "reasons:", followed by the crossed out symbol of the female gender and immediately below, under the horizontal line, there is the word "fulfilled", the abbreviation "wk" (meaning "work"), as well as the word "conditions". In the next sentence the interpreter noted down the surname "Thatcher", placed it in round brackets and crossed it out, which effectively conveys the idea of this additional remark: "They haven't met Margaret Thatcher yet". What follows below is the symbol of "policy", the word "encourage" which has been crossed out, and then two plus signs indicating the idea of "more", the symbol of the female gender and below the horizonal line – the symbol the interpreter adopted for the concept of "the army", i. e. two crossed arrows pointing up.

English original

Women make up about **8%** of the personnel in the **army** and the **navy** in the **United Kingdom. In the United States** which has exactly the same policy as the United Kingdom, women make up as many as **16%** of the armed forces.

Compare that to the situation in Denmark and Norway. Women make up **5%** of the army in **Denmark** and only **3%** in **Norway.**

Screenshot 16

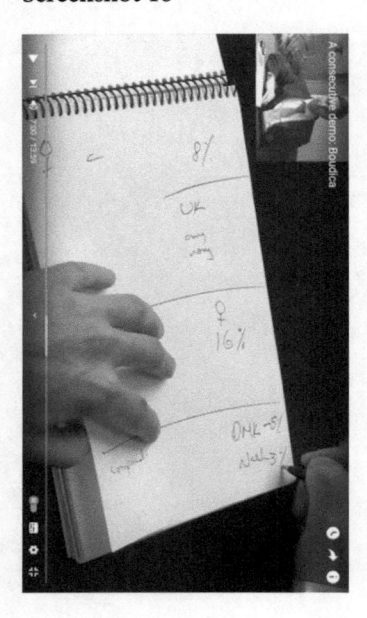

Comments

In the first sentence of this fragment the interpreter noted down the symbol of the female gender, the letter "c" standing for "constitute" (a synonym to the original "make up"), the number "8%" and below the horizontal line the acronym "UK", as well as the terms "army" and "navy". In the following sentence she noted down the acronym "US" (covered in this screenshot by the interpreter's hand), followed by the symbol of the female gender and the number "16%". What stands below is the word "compared", and the abbreviations for the two previously mentioned countries, i.e. "DMK" (Denmark) and "Now" (Norway), with the numbers "5%" and "3%" respectively.

English original
So, what's my **conclusion?** Well, basically, it's this: **if you**'re a **woman** and you **feel** that it's your **inalienable right** as a woman to **serve in the army** in **exactly the same way as a man** might, then **I suggest** that there are two courses of action open to you:

Screenshot 17

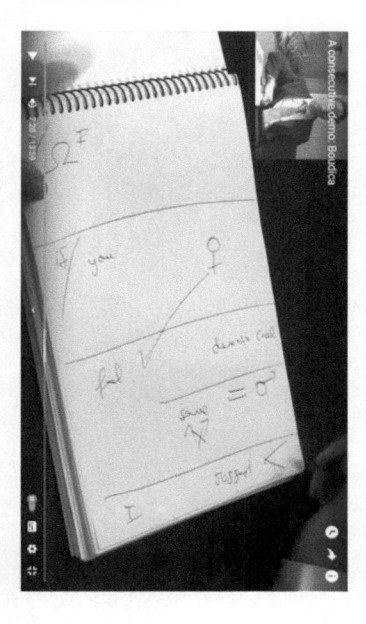

Comments
On top of the page we can see the conjunction "so" and after a diagonal line there is the symbol indicating the concept of "conclusion", i.e. the omega sign (Ω), followed by what looks like the letter "P" (the Spanish "pues", meaning "therefore"). In the next sentence the interpreter noted down the conjunction "if", then the pronoun "you" followed by the symbol of the female gender, and in the following sentence there is the word "feel", the expression "derecho inal." (standing for "inalienable right") and below the horizontal line there is the word "serve" with two crossed arrows underneath, then the equality sign (=) followed by the symbol of the male gender. In the next sentence the interpreter noted down the personal pronoun "I" followed by the verb "suggest" and then the two lines indicating "two courses of action".

English original

if you want to avail yourself of your right to **go to the toilet surrounded by 6 or 7** battle-hardened and probably **sex-starved men, or if** you want to avail yourself of your right to have somebody **charge** at you with a bayonet, screaming as they do so – **then** fine, go ahead and **marry a Norwegian or a Dane**

Screenshot 18

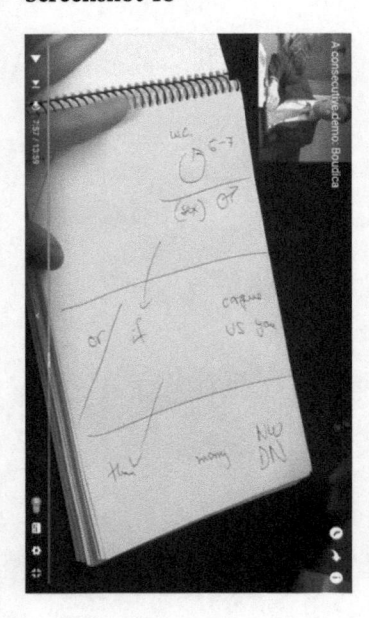

Comments

Here, she noted down the conjunction "if" and after the diagonal line she wrote "W.C.", the round arrow indicating "surrounded by", then the numbers "6–7" and the symbol of the male gender, and below the horizontal line there is the word "sex" placed in round brackets and the symbol of the female gender. In the next sentence there is the conjunction "or" and following the diagonal line – the conjunction "if" followed by the word "cargar" (meaning "to charge"), the abbreviation "US" and the pronoun "you". In the final sentence in this fragment the interpreter noted down the linking word "then", the verb "marry" and the two previously used abbreviations standing for the countries "Norway" and "Denmark".

English original
if, however, you think it might be a little bit more fun to fly **a stealth bomber** –
well, **in that case** perhaps you could consider **marrying an American** instead.
Thank you very much for your attention.

Screenshot 19

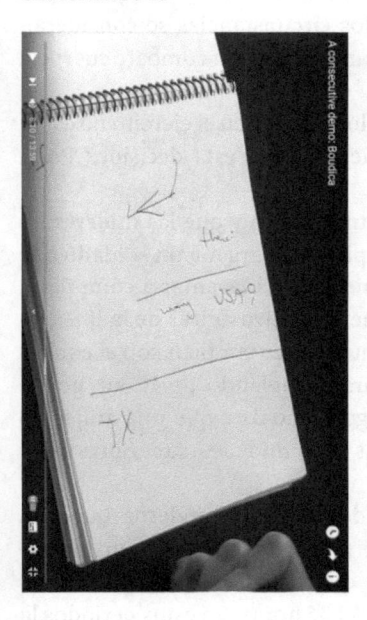

Comments
In the final page we can see the conjunction "if", then the picture of an airplane
immediately underneath (standing for: "a stealth bomber"), and below – the
linking word "then" (standing for the expression "in that case"). Below the
horizontal line there is the verb "marry" followed by the abbreviation "USA" and
the symbol of a person. In the final sentence of the speech the interpreter only
noted down the abbreviation "TX" meaning "thanks".

Spanish translation

Señora Presidenta, Señoras y Señores, buenos días.
Una de las figuras más conocidas de la historia británica es una mujer, con el
nombre de Boudica. Esta mujer era guerrera que vivió hace unos 2000 años y
dirigió un levantamiento contra las topas romanas que ocupaban las Islas Bri-
tánicas an aquel entonces. Era reconocida por su ferocidad ya que no tenía
ningún reparo de cortar cabezas o de clavar lo que en aquel entonces se usó como

un espada, a los soldados romanos. Sorprende que, dado la importancia de Boudica, el gobierno británico haya tomado la decisión de impedir que las mujeres luchen si se trata de un combate cuerpo a cuerpo. Esta decisión se tomó después de una revisión que hiciera el gobierno hace 4 años. Voy a ser muy cuidadoso con mis palabras: no se permite que las mujeres luchen en una situación cuerpo a cuerpo en el frente. Porque está permitido que participen en un combate de artillería o como pilotos – estas dos circunstancias se consideran participar en el frente. Pero la mujer no puede participar en un combate cuerpo a cuerpo contra el enemigo.

El resultado de esta revisión es que el 30 % de los puestos en el ejército no están disponibles para las mujeres. ¿Por qué el gobierno tomó esta decisión? Pues, existen varias razones.

La primera es que la guerra moderna es bastnate física y que las mujeres no tienen la fuerza física que necesitarían por ejemplo para cargar a un soldado que ha caído herido. Si esto fuera la sitiación, uno necesitaría levantar a compñero, que a veces llega a pesar entre 80 o 90 kg, y ponerlo a salvo detrás de la línea de combate. Además de cargar al compañero hay que cargar también con el equipo propio y con él del compañero, entonces estamos hablando de 15 kg, por el equipo de cada uno. Y esto es mucho peso. El gobierno dice que una mujer no tiene la suficiente fuerza, especialmente en las extremidades superiores para cargar con tanto peso.

La segunda razón se debe a la naturaleza de la guerra moderna que está bastante mecanizada, por eso que se utilizan tantos tanques. En un tanque normalmente hay un equipo de 6–7 hombres que tienen que compartir este espacio del interior, a veces por periodos entre 24 y 36 horas. En estos periodos la única posibilidad para ir al baño es usar un retrete químico que está colocado debajo del asiento. El argumento es que ya es bastante vergonzoso que un hombre tenga que hacer sus necesidades enfrente de sus compañeros y sería todavía peor para una mujer.

El tercer argumento es que el hecho de que una mujer tenga que luchar en una situación de cuerpo a cuerpo es bastante experimental. De hecho nadie sabe que pasaría hasta que ocurriece. Nadie sabe que es lo que haría una mujer si de pronto vea un tipo enorme de 2 metros apuntándole con una bayoneta y corriendo hacia ella. A lo mejor cambiaría de idea y, pues, el resultado no sería bueno ya que se pondrían muchas vidas en peligro. No merece la pena simplemente por intenrar tener una política pro mujeres en el ejército.

Hay otros países, sin embargo, que son más flexibles en este respecto. En Dinamarca y en Noruega, se permite que las mujeres combatan en todas las posiciones, incluyendo el combate cuerpo a cuerpo. Esto es comprensible debido a que en estos países hay una larga tradición de igualdad entre hombres y mujeres.

Pero no hay que dejarnos llevar porque aunque las mujeres puedan luchar en todas las líneas de frente, en realidad no lo hacen. ¿Cuáles son las razones? Pues, una de las razones es que se dice que ninguna mujer ha cumplido con todas las condiciones necesarias para el puesto. Esto seguro lo dicen porque no han conocido a Margaret Thatcher. Esta política no anima a que entren más mujeres en las fuerzas armadas. De hecho, en Reino Unido el número de mujeres que sirven en el ejército y en la marina es del 8 %. En Estados Unidos, un país que tiene unas políticas similares, el número de mujeres es del 16 %.

Comparemos estas cifras con Dinamarca donde las fuerzas femeninas componen un 5 %, o Noruega donde componen un 3 %.

¿Cuál sería mi conclusión entonces? Pues, que si usted es mujer y que siente que tiene el derecho inalienable de servir en el ejército de la misma manera que un hombre, le sugiero dos alternativas:

1. Por un lado, si no le importa hacer sus necesidades delante de un equipo de 6 o 7 hombres sudorosos y hambrientos de sexo, pues, adelante. Si, por otro lado, tampoco le importa que un tipo enorme cargue contra usted, entonces puede usted casarse con un noruego o con un danés.
2. Si, por otro lado, preferiría ser piloto de guerra, entonces mejor le sugiero que se case con un estadounidense.

Muchas gracias.

Back translation into English

Madam President, Ladies and Gentlemen, good morning.
One of the best-known figures in the British history is a woman, by the name of Boudica. This woman was a warrior who lived about 2000 years ago and led an uprising against the Roman troops who occupied the British Isles at the time. She was renowned for her ferocity as she had no qualms about cutting off heads or stabbing what was then used as a sword into Roman soldiers. It is surprising that, given the importance of Boudica, the British government has taken the decision to prevent women from fighting if it is a close combat. This decision was made after a review by the government 4 years ago. I am going to be very careful with my words: women are not allowed to fight in a hand-to-hand situation on the front lines. But they are allowed to participate in artillery combat or as pilots – these two circumstances are considered the front line. But the woman cannot engage in a close combat against the enemy.

The result of this review is that 30% of positions in the military are not available to women. Why did the government make this decision? Well, there are several reasons.

The first one is that modern warfare is quite physical and that women do not have the physical strength they would need, for example, to carry a wounded soldier. If this were the situation, one would need to lift a comrade, who sometimes weighs between 80 and 90 kg, and carry him safely behind the line of combat. In addition to carrying your partner, you also have to carry your own equipment and that of your partner, so we are talking about 15 kg, for each equipment. And this is a lot of weight. The government says that a woman does not have enough strength, especially in the upper limbs to carry so much weight.

The second reason is due to the very mechanized nature of modern warfare, which is why so many tanks are used. In a tank there is normally a team of 6–7 men who have to share this space inside, sometimes for periods between 24 and 36 hours. In these periods the only possibility to go to the bathroom is to use a chemical toilet that is placed under the seat. The argument is that it is embarrassing enough that a man has to relieve himself in front of his companions and it would be even worse for a woman.

The third argument is that the situation in which a woman would have to fight hand-to-hand is quite experimental. In fact, nobody knows what would happen until it happens. No one knows what a woman would do if she suddenly saw a huge 2-meter tall guy pointing a bayonet at her and running towards her. Maybe she would change her mind and, well, the result would not be good since many lives would be put at risk. It's not worth it just to try to have a pro-women policy in the military.

There are other countries, however, that are more flexible in this respect. In Denmark and Norway, women are allowed to fight in all positions, including hand-to-hand combat. This is understandable because in these countries there is a long tradition of equality between men and women.

But we must not get carried away because although women can fight on all front lines, in reality they do not. What are the reasons? Well, one of the reasons is that it is said that no woman has fulfilled all the necessary conditions for the position. They say this surely because they have not met Margaret Thatcher. This policy does not encourage more women to enter the armed forces. In fact, in the UK the number of women serving in the army and navy is 8%. In the United States, a country that has similar policies, the number of women is 16%.

Compare these figures with Denmark where female forces make up 5%, or Norway where they make up 3%.

What would be my conclusion then? Well, if you are a woman and you feel that you have the inalienable right to serve in the military in the same way as a man, I suggest two alternatives:

1. On the one hand, if you don't mind relieving yourself in front of a team of 6 or 7 sweaty, sex-hungry men, then go for it. If, on the other hand, you don't mind

being charged at by a huge guy either, then you can marry a Norwegian or a Dane.

2. If, on the other hand, you'd rather be a fighter pilot, then I suggest you marry an American.

Thank you very much.

Additional comments and conclusions

What is immediately striking, when looking at this interpreter's notes, is that she was following the vertical system of note-taking, i. e. instead of writing from left to right, the notes go from top of the page to the bottom. Every single sentence is separated from another with a horizontal line stretching throughout the whole width of the page. This manner of note-taking allows one to introduce a clear structure which later facilitates the interpretation process.

The analysis demonstrated that this particular interpreter was using two languages when taking notes, both English and Spanish, as well as various shortened forms of words, acronyms and numbers. She was also using symbols, both the ones that are already quite popular among the interpreters like the symbol of a decision or of a person, as well as the established symbols derived from fields of science such as biology (the symbol of the male and the female genders). However, the interpreter was also creating her own symbols such as one for "Madam Chair" which was a simple drawing of a chair as a piece of furniture, the crossed arrows indicating the concept of "the army" or a simple picture of an airplane symbolizing "a stealth bomber".

In order to mark the links between concepts, the interpreter was using shorter horizontal lines, above which she was noting down a symbol, a word or an abbreviation standing for one concept, and immediately below a symbol, a word or an abbreviation standing for another, closely related to the upper one. She was also using longer arrows to indicate links between individual sentences.

What is also important was that she was always writing down the linking words and the conjunctions. Although these words do not appear to be particularly significant, definitely not as much as the content words, they play a crucial role in the entire discourse and they allow the interpreter to form logical links between the sentences, as well as introduce a clear cause-and-effect structure.

Although the target language text produced on the basis of those notes is shorter and omitted a few remarks mentioned in the original one, the interpreter successfully preserved the overall message, as well as all the crucial details. When interpreting on the basis of her notes, she was very fluent and clearly had no problems deciphering the notes, as well as she had no doubts as to what the individual symbols or abbreviations meant. She managed to produce a very fluent and successful translation of the English original, largely due to the good-quality and reliable notes she had taken beforehand. The analysis illustrates the importance of developing a good and reliable note-taking system which is crucial to performing a successful consecutive interpretation.

Chapter 4:
Interpreting as a Process

4.1 Techniques and Strategies in Interpreting

Teresa Tomaszkiewicz, who translated and adapted the book *Terminologie de la traduction* (Polish: "Terminologia tłumaczenia"), provides a clear and very approachable distinction between the terms which tend to be confused within the area of Translation Studies, namely: a translation technique and a translation strategy, stating that a translation technique is:

> "the translator's approach to specific elements in the source text with the purpose of achieving equivalence in the target text. Unlike the translation strategy, which determines the translator's global behaviour in relation to a specific text, translation techniques are individual decisions regarding individual text segments, analysed in a micro-context" (Tomaszkiewicz 2006, 95).[40]

When discussing techniques and strategies in the context of interpreting and the resultant confusion between the terms, Tryuk (2010, 182) refers to the distinction provided by Zabalbeascoa (2000, 119–122) who defined these two notions in the following way:
- a technique is an ability to be used in accordance with a certain procedure (just like with playing a musical instrument or painting); the selection of a translation technique requires looking at the source text and deciding which of its components are the most relevant for conveying the intended message, and hence necessary to be translated, and, afterwards, selecting the best and the most convenient way of rendering each of these constituent parts;
- a strategy is a pattern of behaviour intended to solve a certain problem or achieving a specific goal; it is considered a translator's conscious action aimed

---

40 "sposób postępowania tłumacza w stosunku do konkretnych elementów tekstu wyjściowego w celu zachowania ekwiwalencji w tekście docelowym. W odróżnieniu od strategii tłumaczenia, która determinuje postępowanie globalne tłumacza w stosunku do określonego tekstu, techniki tłumaczeniowe są decyzjami jednostkowymi, dotyczącymi poszczególnych segmentów tekstu, analizowanych w mikrokontekście" (author's own translation).

at improving his/her efficiency and effectiveness when performing a given task (Zabalbeascoa 2000, 119–122, after Tryuk 2010, 182).

What seems to follow from the above explanations, particularly in the interpreting context, is that a technique is a more narrow term, indicating an individual decision aimed at solving a certain problem concerning a particular interpreting unit, or, as observed by Tryuk (2010, 182), "an existing problem at the level of interpreting unit". As she states, interpreting techniques are applied when the source text is too dense and information-packed, or when the speaker uses terminology with which the interpreter is unfamiliar, or in a situation when the speaker delivers the speech at too fast a pace, or with a foreign accent, and, in consequence, the interpreter may find it difficult to distinguish separate interpreting units.

Gile (2009, 216–227) divides interpretation techniques (which he calls "tactics"[41]) into the following categories:

1. Comprehension techniques (applied when comprehension problems occur):
   - delaying the response – when comprehension problems arise, the interpreter may delay their response for up to a few seconds so that they have time to think while more information is coming from the discourse being heard. This may help significantly and solve the comprehension problem. However, the hidden cost of this technique is that it entails the necessity to accumulate information in the short-term memory and hence running the risk of losing certain speech components;
   - reconstructing the component in the context – sometimes the interpreter may not have properly heard or understood a certain term, name, number, etc., and he/she might attempt to reconstruct it relying on their general knowledge of the subject, of the language, as well as of the situation (i. e. the extralinguistic knowledge). Such a reconstruction is also something that people use, largely subconsciously, in everyday situations when trying to understand what others want to convey. However, when used consciously in an interpreting situation, it is considered a separate technique. If applied successfully, reconstruction may lead to a full recovery of information. As a downside, it may also involve some waiting time until more information is available;

---

41 Gile uses the term "tactics" to refer to "deliberate decisions and actions aimed at preventing or solving problems, as opposed to spontaneous, perhaps unconscious reactions" (2009, 201). Since the specific "tactics" that he proposes and that are discussed in this chapter concern the interpreter's decisions regarding individual text segments, rather than the interpreter's global behaviour in relation to an entire text, I decided, for the sake of clarity and consistency of terms, and following Tomaszkiewicz's distinction between "a technique" and a "strategy" presented above, to refer to them as "techniques".

- using the boothmate's help – in simultaneous interpreting there are typically at least two interpreters in the booth at the same time, with one of them actively interpreting and the other passively listening. The passive colleague may pay their full attention to listening and, therefore, have a better chance of understanding some more challenging speech parts than the active interpreter who needs to divide their attention between listening to the input and producing the output. Also, the passive interpreter has time to consult some resources (such as a dictionary or a document relevant to the speech), thus providing assistance to the active colleague (usually in writing). Therefore, the presence of such a passive partner in the booth during an interpreting job can be of major help for any interpreter. If the two interpreters have spent some time working with each other and have learnt to read each other's non-verbal signals, they can communicate successfully by means of body language and sense each other's hesitation or doubts, anticipate the problem before it arises and act in order to prevent it. Sometimes even simply writing down a single word, a number or a name by the passive colleague may immensely help the active interpreter if they have not heard it properly. This combined effort of two interpreters may significantly facilitate their job, as well as notably improve the quality and efficiency of their performance;
- consulting resources – if the interpreter is working alone, they may try to consult the resources available, such as documents that have been provided in advance. If those have been studied prior to the conference, preferably with the most important vocabulary and phrases highlighted in the text, finding the relevant term during the conference should not pose a problem. Hence, the importance of document preparation and its effective management. Compiling a glossary of terms, as well as writing down the crucial names and facts to be mentioned during the conference, and having these close at hand, can also be of invaluable help. An alternative solution to paper documents and notes is having a small laptop in the booth where all these can be stored and accessed readily and comfortably and, with the Internet connection, the interpreter will also have access to all sorts of reference materials, dictionaries and a plethora of other resources. However, since this process is certainly time-consuming, it is best left to the passive interpreter in the booth rather than the active one, or, if there is only one interpreter in the booth, they may use some idle moments, ones in which they are not interpreting actively, in order to consult resources.
2. Preventive techniques (applied to prevent problems that may arise as a result of time pressure or limited processing capacity):
   - note-taking – as indicated in the previous chapter, when the discourse features certain numbers, proper names, dates, etc. that interpreters may

forget before they start rendering the speech into the target language, it is useful to note them down in order to aid the memory later on and not waste its capacity; however, as rightly observed by Gile (2009, 204), this technique costs time and increases the risk of losing other vital information coming right before or after the item that has just been written down;

- lengthening or shortening the Ear-Voice Span (EVS) – EVS is "the time lag between the moment a speech segment is heard and its reformulation in the target language" (Gile 2009, 204). By varying it, interpreters may control (to a certain extent) processing capacity requirements, for instance, shortening the lag may reduce short-term memory requirements. However, this comes at the expense of decreased anticipation potential and increased risk of misunderstanding the sentence. On the other hand, increasing the time lag may improve comprehension but may overload short-term memory;

- segmentation and unloading of short-term memory – in a situation when the two languages exhibit considerable syntactic differences or the sentence structures are unclear, the interpreter may decide to reformulate speech segments even before they fully find out what the speaker wants to say. When doing so, they may use neutral sentence beginnings, for instance if the interpreter is faced with a sentence expressing a casual relationship like: "Because of the complex character of equation (2) as shown above, compounded by the difficulty of finding a unique solution to equations (3) and (4) which correspond to a steady state system ...", they may reformulate it in the target language as follows: "Equation (2) as shown above is complex, equations (3) and (4) describe a steady system, it is difficult to find a unique solution to them ..." (Gile 2009, 205). This technique can relieve the short-term memory;

- changing the order of elements in a list – lists or other enumerations are high-density segments which significantly burden the short-term memory. This technique implies changing the order of the elements provided so that the last ones are mentioned first (which frees memory from the information), before moving on to the remaining elements. As observed by Gile (ibidem), this reduces memory effort load and works best with names or easily transcoded terms;

3. Reformulation techniques – some of them are exactly the same as comprehension techniques, such as: delaying the response, using the boothmate's help or consulting the resources; however, there are some additional ones:

- replacing a segment with a superordinate term or a more general segment – if the interpreter is unable to fully comprehend a certain speech segment or reproduce it in the target language, they may try to reformulate the message in a less accurate manner by using a superordinate term (if the problem concerns a single word), or by formulating a more general segment (if the problem concerns a clause or an entire sentence), for instance: "Monsieur Stephen Wedgeworth" may be reformulated as "the speaker", and "DEC, IBM, Hewlett Packard et Texas Instruments" as "a number of computer vendors" (Gile 2009, 206). Although this technique entails information loss, this loss may not always be significant as the same information might be repeated throughout the speech, or may be already known to the audience;

- explaining or paraphrasing – sometimes, even though the interpreter understands a term, it may happen that they do not have an accurate equivalent readily available in the target language. In such a situation, they may decide to explain or describe it rather than translate it. An advantage of this technique is that it allows the interpreter to convey the necessary information. On the other hand, it necessitates more time and processing capacity. Also, by resorting to it, the interpreter may run the risk of having their credibility undermined as the audience realizes he/she does not know the appropriate term in the target language;
- reproducing the sound heard in the source-language speech – if the interpreter does not know a name or term mentioned in the source language speech, they may try to reproduce the sound as heard. This technique might work well when the audience knows the name or term and may automatically hear it in its correct pronunciation, not even realizing that the interpreter encountered a problem. However, there is a risk that the interpreter's sound approximation is not good enough, and the problem is detected by the listeners, which, in turn, may undermine the interpreter's reputation;
- "instant naturalization" – if the interpreter does not know the equivalent term in the target language, they may choose to naturalize the source-language term by adapting it to the morphological and/or phonological rules of the target language. For example, the French term "télédétection" (remote sensing) may be translated into English as "teledetection" (Gile 2009, 207). This technique may be very effective when the two languages involved are morphologically similar or when there are a lot of borrowings from the source language in the target language (as in the case of the IT field where English is a loan language for most non-English speaking countries). The end effect is that the interpreter, in a sense, "invents" terms that actually function in the target language, so they should not strike the listeners as odd;
- transcoding – this technique entails a word-for-word translation of the source language term or speech segment into the target language. Just like the previously mentioned technique, this one may also prove useful when encountering lexical problem since, just like in "instant naturalization", the interpreter may arrive at the already existing target language terms. And

even when the interpreter produces a term which does not function in the target language, it may still facilitate comprehension for the listeners due to the semantic similarity;

– form-based interpreting – the conference interpreting community appears to agree that it is the meaning and not the form that should be the priority for interpreters and that they should focus on the meaning rather than try to find direct linguistic equivalents. This approach leads to better comprehension of the speaker's intentions and better reformulation of the message in the target language, as well as reduced linguistic interference. Nevertheless, in certain situations, for instance when fatigue sets in, or the source language speech is very fast, the interpreter may apply the so-called "form-based interpreting" (Dam 2001, after Gile 2009, 209), whereby they are guided by the source language words and syntax when producing the target language speech. A significant drawback of this technique, however, are losses in terms of idiomaticity and clarity; however, in some situations it may prove effective in preserving more information from the source speech than meaning-based interpreting;

– informing the listeners of a problem – if the interpreter missed an important piece of information, they may decide to openly admit this to the listeners by saying, for example: "… and an author whose name the interpreter did not catch," or "… the interpreter is sorry, s/he missed the last number" (Gile 2009, 209). In such a situation it may happen that the listeners will request the speaker to clarify or repeat some information. As observed by Gile (ibidem), this technique is not applied frequently since it is time-consuming and it draws the audience's attention to the interpreter's problems and this, in turn, may undermine the interpreter's credibility and reputation. Hence, this technique is recommended only when the piece of information missed is really significant;

– referring the listeners to another information source – during conferences, information is imparted to the listeners not only via the speaker's words, but also in the form of handouts and slides displayed on screen, overhead transparencies and online presentations. Therefore, if faced with comprehension or interpretation problems, the interpreter may always refer the audience to the data presented on one of these media, which is a useful and convenient technique;

– omitting a speech segment – the interpreter may decide to omit information unconsciously simply because they did not have enough capacity available for listening, processing and rendering a certain speech segment at a given moment. Omission may also occur as a result of the interpreter being unable to hold the speech segment in their short-term memory long enough to render it to the target language. However, the omission technique might be the interpreter's deliberate choice when they decide not to translate a certain piece of information provided in the source language speech. This may occur when this particular piece of information is not really relevant to the overall message, or it has relatively little value when compared to other information which might be lost if the interpreter paid too much attention to rendering this less important piece. This technique may also be applied if the speaker said something inappropriate and the interpreter feels that translating it would either harm the speaker's interests or jeopardize the intended outcome of the meeting. However, contrary to a popular belief, omission does not necessarily entail a loss of information as the listeners may receive it elsewhere in the speech or it may be already known to them. Nevertheless, this is still a risky technique and should not be chosen too often, as "[i]t is unethical to omit deliberately important information without informing the listeners of the loss, and some interpreters (and clients) may challenge the legitimacy of the tactic in all cases and question the interpreter's ability to judge what is important and what isn't" (Gile 2009, 210). Still, one needs to bear in mind that, for instance in court interpreting, a decision to omit a segment would be unethical (even if the interpreter deemed this particular segment as inappropriate) due to the norms involved.[42] However, in diplomatic meetings between people coming from different cultural backgrounds, omission or attenuation of an inappropriate comment or joke may be justified for the sake of avoiding a serious diplomatic blunder;

- "parallel" reformulation – this technique might be applied when the interpreting conditions are especially bad, the interpreter is unable to comprehend and/or accurately render the source language segment, but they feel they need to continue speaking. Hence, they may invent a speech segment compatible with the rest of the speaker's statement. However, this technique is very risky and only to be used in exceptional cases, and with caution, only in situations when the continuity in speech is of paramount importance, rather than the content (which might be the case, as Gile (2009, 211) observes, in some TV shows);

- turning off the microphone – this technique is described by Gile (ibidem) as another "extreme" one, which is nowadays largely unacceptable to clients. The only situation in which it actually might be applied is when working conditions for the interpreting are so bad that the interpreter is

---

convinced they are unable to do any useful work at all, which means that continuing to interpret would be worse than providing no interpreting at all. However, this is a very extreme situation and even if the conditions are bad, the interpreters typically continue interpreting, trying to do their best, sometimes informing the listeners honestly about the situation and indicating that they are incapable of ensuring good-quality interpreting in these conditions.

All the above-mentioned techniques concerned interpreters' decisions regarding individual speech segments or individual interpretation problems and the ways of solving them. However, there are also more general approaches concerning the interpreter's global behaviour in relation to the entire speech text, and these can be referred to as "interpreting strategies". Tryuk (2010, 182) states that in the field of interpreting,

> "strategy means such interpreter's behaviour that enables him to make the complex mental effort resulting from simultaneous listening and speaking when both source and target texts are produced only once, as a rule without any possibility to listen again. In addition the interpreter cannot verify nor even self-correct his/her performance. The whole interpreting operation is conducted under time pressure and stress. Strategies, as overall interpreter's behaviour, always appear, although they can be realized to a different extent, depending on the interpreter's professional experience".

Tryuk (2010, 186) also observes that, as regards interpreting, a strategy should be distinguished on the basis of its characteristic features, specific to this particular field, i.e.:
- simultaneous listening and speaking;
- time pressure;
- strong reliance on one's short term memory.

Therefore, she enumerates three main interpreting strategies (2010, 186–191):
1. Anticipation strategy – this strategy enables the interpreter to listen and speak simultaneously. Anticipation is based on the interpreter's linguistic, semantic, contextual, situational and thematic knowledge (Wilss 1978, after Tryuk 2010, 186). However, the mechanism of anticipation occurs not only in interpreting. In fact, experts in psycholinguistics view it as one of the basic mechanisms of perception and speech production. In verbal communication anticipation entails predicting what the speaker is going to say, based on certain linguistic (grammatical and lexical), and non-linguistic elements. This is also what happens in interpreting – using this strategy the interpreter anticipates the yet unheard speech parts. Although these predictions may turn out false, "they activate cognitive processes in the receiver's brain, directing the processes of

comprehending the message" (Tryuk 2010, 187). It also allows the interpreter to reconstruct the message elements. Anticipation mechanism is particularly important in conference interpreting where the interpreter has to comprehend the source language message and simultaneously reproduce it in the target language – anticipation allows them to understand the message in the shortest time possible. When using this strategy, the interpreter tries to predict the incoming speech elements based on the already heard elements. Anticipation works not only on the level of semantics, but also on phonological, morphological and syntactic levels and functions thanks to the phenomenon of redundancy which means that one piece of information is repeated in different forms several times throughout the speech. "Redundancy enables the receiver to formulate a hypothesis about an utterance and compare it with the models stored in memory, where the patterns of linguistic behaviour, updated by perception, are coded" (ibidem). In the anticipation strategy the interpreter activates both the bottom-up mechanism, processing the acoustic level first and then moving on to the lexical, syntactic, and semantic levels; as well as the top-down mechanism, in which they formulate hypotheses about the message, based on their knowledge and expectation. While discussing the anticipation strategy, Tryuk (ibidem) refers to the interpretive theory proposed by Seleskovitch (1978), who distinguished two kinds of knowledge indispensable for this strategy: linguistic, i. e. the knowledge of certain vocabulary and grammatical rules, and extralinguistic which entails the knowledge of the subject matter and the communicative situation. Tryuk (2010, 188) also mentions a model of anticipation developed by Chernov (1994), which assumes the simultaneous functioning of anticipation at all levels. If the interpreter knows the speaker, they already activate the predicting process concerning the situation. Here anticipation starts at a higher level and is related with top-down processing. Then, it moves on to the level of sound and corresponds to bottom-up processing, and then to syntactic and semantic levels. However, in a situation when the interpreter does not know the speaker, this happens the other way round – anticipation begins at the level of sound, and then the interpreter creates a general plan of the speech. The model proposed by Chernov assumes the existence of the so-called inferences during interpreting, which are determined by the level of mastering the source language by the interpreter, their cognitive knowledge, situational knowledge, as well as the knowledge of the sender. Hence, there are:
– linguistic inferences, which are based on the verbal form of the message and its linguistic meaning;
– cognitive inferences, which happen when semantic components of the speech part interact with the interpreter's previous knowledge;

- situational inferences, which are connected with the meaning of an utterance and the situational context.

As neatly summed up by Tryuk (2010, 189), the anticipation strategy offers the following advantages for the interpreter:

- it reduces the interpreting time and decreases the amount of information;
- it reduces the energy required for interpreting;
- it increases accuracy of comprehension.

2. Condensation strategy – it is used at the stage of text production and entails reducing information while interpreting, which is possible due to the redundancy phenomenon. According to the studies conducted by Alexieva (1983, after Tryuk 2010, 190), in order for successful communication in simultaneous interpreting, the interpreter should produce a target language text that would have a greater semantic load and be shorter than the original one. This is possible thanks to the mechanism of compression, and compression can be achieved by means of, for instance, omissions, substitutions and encapsulations. Also Dam (1993, after Tryuk 2010, 190) claims that if the interpreter is unable to note down the entire utterance in the reception stage or to remember the message, condensation should be applied as it allows the transmission of the meaning:

> "Condensation consists of the pronominal or lexical substitution, omission of elements expressing propositional context (known and redundant), omission of elements expressing non-propositional content (phatic and metalinguistic function), and finally omission of expressions of attitude" (Dam 1993, 300–310, after Tryuk 2010, 190).

3. Notation strategy[43] – this strategy allows the interpreter to overcome the limitations of their short-term memory. During the process of note-taking, the interpreter listens to and analyzes the original text at the same time, as well as notes down information using words, abbreviations, symbols, etc. The note-taking technique allows the interpreter to store information and then use it when interpreting the message into the target language. One significant advantage of note-taking is memory support and enhancement of the listening process (Ilg and Lambert 1996, 78, after Tryuk 2010, 191). However, it should be pointed out that the notes cannot replace the process of interpretation. The interpreter does not (since this would be virtually impossible) note down the entire utterance or the whole sentence, nor do they write down random words or draw pictures. However, the notes they take always reflect the information they have just heard and are supposed to reflect the sequence of logically-structured information built up in a coherent manner. The in-

---

43 More detailed information on this particular strategy can be found in Chapter 3.

terpreter always listens carefully to the source language segment and decides what should be noted down, with the notes always designated for a single and immediate use, thus being an auxiliary strategy supporting the listening process and the speech comprehension. Also, the interpreter is aware of the fact that note-taking may help them overcome an interpreting problem, resulting from, for instance, memory's shortcomings during listening or a problem with processing the message in the source language. However, it is crucial (and this also comes with practice) that the interpreter knows "what to note, when to note, how to note, in what form to note (by using symbols, drawings, abbreviations, etc.), in what language to note and finally how to read the notes" (Tryuk 2010, 191). When note-taking is mastered by the interpreter, this strategy may improve comprehension and contribute to the interpreter's successful performance.

The techniques and strategies discussed above constitute a sort of a "toolkit", from which the interpreter may select one or more, depending on the situation, the speakers, the audience, the purpose of the meeting, etc. Although not all of these techniques and strategies may come in handy during the interpreter's career, he/she may still find comfort in the thought that they have a wide range of tools at their disposal and may reach for any of them, should the need arise.

However, techniques and strategies are not the only aspects that the interpreters should be aware of. They also have to realize that communication is not only about verbal language. In fact, a lot of information, whether in day-to-day communication or in an interpreting setting, is conveyed by means of non-verbal signals and these will be discussed in the following section.

4.2   Non-verbal Elements

When discussing elements involved in the interpreting activity, Miletich (2015, 169) points out that a lot of people would view interpreting simply as stating in one language what is being said in another. This, however, would imply that this activity involves verbal language only. Therefore, he quotes the definition suggested by Poyatos (2002, 271), whereby interpreting is:

"The relaying from a speaker-actor to a listener-viewer (or audience) of verbal and nonverbal messages indistinctively through verbal and nonverbal ones, as dictated by the synonymous, antonymous or absent verbal or nonverbal signs with respect to each other's communication systems".

This definition draws the reader's attention to the fact that interpreting involves also non-verbal language. This language encompasses gestures, facial expressions, posture, eye contact,[44] as well as paralanguage which is defined as:

> "the vocal but nonverbal elements of communication by speech. Paralanguage includes not only suprasegmental features of speech, such as tone and stress, but also such factors as volume and speed of delivery, voice quality, hesitations, and nonlinguistic sounds, such as sighs, whistles, or groans."[45]

The elements mentioned in the above definition are referred to as paralinguistic cues or paralinguistic features, and they can be crucial to the meaning of an utterance. They may provide clues regarding the speaker's mood, convey the fact that he/she is angry or sarcastic, which may not always be obvious merely from the words he/she is uttering. Example elements of non-verbal signals are presented below.

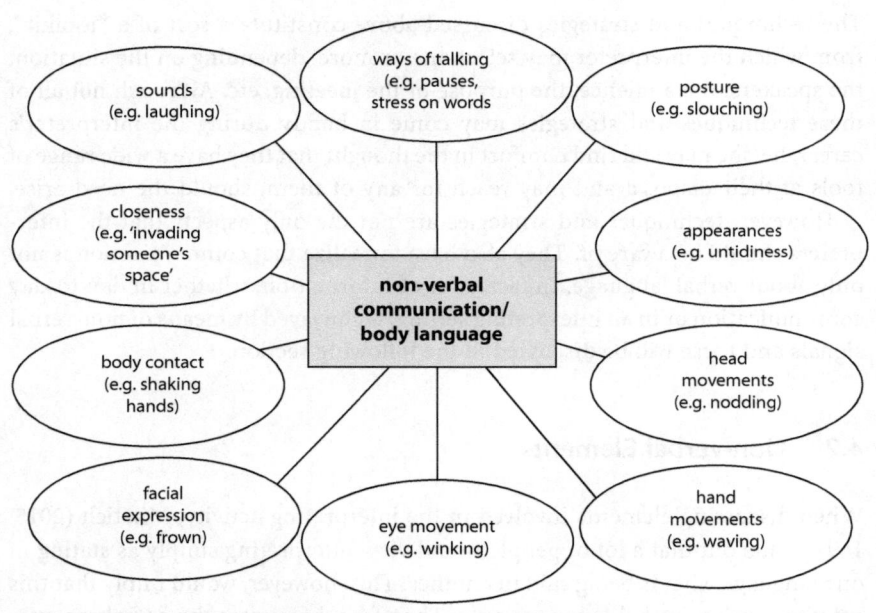

Picture 1: Elements of non-verbal communication (source: https://sites.google.com/site/comm unicationskill4you/non-verbal-communication, accessed 11.03.2023).

As observed by Tryuk (2007, 119), all the non-verbal signals allow people to better express their emotions, thus facilitating communication. In the interpreting

---

44 The study of body movements, gestures, facial expressions, etc., as a means of communication is called kinesics (https://www.dictionary.com/browse/kinesics, accessed 11.03.2023).
45 https://dictionary.apa.org/paralanguage, accessed 11.03.2023.

setting these elements play a very significant role. They may indicate a repetition of the verbal message, or may complement or strengthen it. Sometimes they may replace a part of the verbal message, for instance when the chair of the meeting uses a gesture to point to the next speaker, and so they allow for a faster transfer of information or overcoming memory problems, for example inability to quickly find the accurate equivalent. Hence, interpreters should always pay careful attention to the speaker's non-verbal signals. However, this is not always easy to do, since, for example in simultaneous interpreting the speaker may not be clearly visible for the interpreter. On top of that, interpreters should not only be aware of non-verbal cues, but also be able to correctly recognize their meaning, which may vary from culture to culture. Only then could they decide if and how those elements should be transferred into the target language. They may, for instance, choose to verbally describe or clarify the speaker's behaviour or use other non-verbal behaviour (Tryuk 2007, 119–120). To illustrate this, Marković (2017, 16) provides an example of the "OK gesture", which is considered offensive in some parts of the world, and for which the interpreter might emphasize the positive aspects of the original message to achieve a similar effect. As a result, the target language audience will not only see the gesture, but also hear the interpretation of its meaning and thus would understand the speaker's intended message. Also, the interpreters need to be conscious of the fact that certain gestures may be misleading for certain cultures or may be used "the other way round", as is the case with the reversal of head nodding for "yes" and head shaking for "no" (Rennert 2008, 210).

Transfer of non-verbal elements is determined by the function they have in the speaker's utterance. If they constitute a repetition or illustration of the verbally expressed message, the interpreter may choose to omit them. However, if these elements replace or strengthen the verbal content, or complement it with extra information, the interpreter should render them into the target language.

Marković (2017, 16) points out that, according to the description of a simultaneous interpreter's job provided by the International Association of Conference Interpreters (AIIC), this kind of interpreter "sits in a booth, listens to the speaker in one language through headphones, and immediately speaks their interpretation into a microphone in another language" (2011, after Marković 2017, 16). As regards the interpreter's kinesic behaviour, this definition emphasizes its two man aspects: since the interpreter is in a booth, in a sitting position, his/her body movements are significantly limited, even though they may still move their head, arms and feet. Besides, the definition quoted, as observed by Marković (ibidem), does not include any information about the visual input during interpretation. As already mentioned, it is very important for the interpreter to be able to see the speaker while interpreting as this visual input provides a plethora of vital information, and this concerns not only the speaker's appearance, mood, or attitude, but also the immediate feedback on the message. Rennert (2008, 216) claims that the lack of visual input in simultaneous interpretation causes more stress for the interpreter and generates the feeling of missing out on information. Interestingly enough, however, this visual input is largely received and processed unconsciously by the interpreter and it may have an impact of the interpreter's comprehension of the message without the interpreter's even being aware of it (ibidem).

The role of the non-verbal elements and the necessity to convey them during interpreting is also emphasized by Piotr Krasnowolski – a translator and interpreter from Kraków, who became famous all over Poland in 2015, when he interpreted during the 17th International Chopin Piano Competition in Poland and his performance of interpreting a 3-minute improvised speech by the chairman of the competition jury, became a sensation. Not only did he do it fluently and flawlessly, without pauses, but he also perfectly conveyed the intended message as well as the emotions of the chairwoman.[46] In the interview that was held with him afterwards in Radio Kraków,[47] he said:

> "People expect to receive the speaker's message plus emotions. Emotions do not cost me a single extra second: I can, for instance, modulate my voice, I can smile... [...] I also understand that I just have to be as invisible as possible, but still need to translate all emotions."[48]

Hence, it seems that emotional intelligence is indispensable for every professional interpreter. As indicated in Krasnowolski's quote, the speaker's emotions, whether expressed consciously or subconsciously, may be interpreted by means of the interpreter's paralanguage. As regards the speakers' conscious emotions (such as irony, humour, admiration, respect), the interpreter might choose to render them either via verbal or paralinguistic means. However, this is not necessarily the case with unconsciously expressed emotions (like embarrassment, insecurity, shock), for which, first of all, the interpreter needs to decide which of them are "ethically permissible" to convey to the target language audience in a particular situation, in order not to invade the speaker's privacy (Poyatos 1997, 255). For instance, the interpreter might decide not to mimic the speaker's nervousness, if he/she decides it would be inappropriate.

---

46 His performance, as well as the entire gala and main prize winner's concert can be viewed at: https://www.youtube.com/watch?v=d3aU6DsWbts.

47 The interview can be watched at: https://www.radiokrakow.pl/wideo/tlumacz-z-krakowa-g wiazda-konkursu-chopinowskiego.

48 "Ludzie mają dostać gołe informacje, plus emocje. Emocje nie kosztują mnie ani jednej dodatkowej sekundy – mogę modulować głos, mogę się uśmiechnąć... [...] Potrafię zrozumieć to, że mam po prostu być jak najmniej widzialny, ale mam przetłumaczyć wszystkie emocje". (Author's own translation).

However, apart from the culturally-conditioned differences in terms of the body languages, such as ones mentioned above, in general, the majority of the speaker's non-verbal signals and kinesic behaviour is understood by the audience, even though this understanding might be subconscious. Hence, it often turns out redundant for the interpreter to verbally or paralinguistically express those cues. Therefore, such non-verbal elements as smiling, shrugging, waving, scratching, arm-crossing, nodding etc., are usually omitted in the interpretation process as they tend to be clear for the listeners, with the interpreter focusing on transmitting the verbal elements of the message (Marković 2017, 22).

The importance of body language and other non-verbal signals so far has been concerning the context of simultaneous interpreting. However, it plays perhaps an even greater role in the consecutive mode since, unlike in the simultaneous one, here even more attention is paid to body language and kinesics. This is because in the consecutive mode the interpreter, in a sense, becomes a speaker, being physically present in the communicative situation and no longer just a medium to deliver the message. Now, he/she is clearly visible for the audience (and not only heard, as is the case in simultaneous interpreting), the significance of their non-verbal behaviour rises, particularly in the production stage (not so much during the note-taking phase). Because the interpreter is visible for the listeners, he/she can use his/her body language to communicate the message in the same manner that the speaker does (Marković 2017, 24). As *Practical Guide for Professional Conference Interpreters* (2016)[49] advises:

> "In consecutive, it is all the more important to be a good public speaker. Don't forget to make eye contact with the audience, and make sure to project poise and confidence with your body language. All the principles of quality interpreting apply, with the additional requirements of the visual dimension and non-verbal performance factors".

During the note-taking stage, the interpreter assumes a rather passive role and hence his/her body position and movement is of a minor importance. He/she is simply focused on listening and taking notes, adopting a posture that they find most comfortable in this situation. However, their body movement should change immediately when they enter the active phase, i.e. the actual interpreting. One of the crucial aspects here is eye contact. Interpreters should mainly look at their listeners, instead of their notes. This is of utmost importance since eye contact serves as a builder of trust, as well as an indicator of interest, if there is no eye contact, or if it is scarce, the audience may have a feeling that the interpreter is untrustworthy and thus his/her credibility may be significantly undermined. Therefore, interpreters who only look at their notes will not make a favourable

---

49 https://aiic.org/document/547/AIICWebzine_Apr2004_2_Practical_guide_for_professional _conference_interpreters_EN.pdf, accessed 11.03.2023.

impression on the listeners and may even come across as unwilling to communicate (Marković 2017, 27–28).

The *Practical Guide for Professional Conference Interpreters* (2016) also advises the interpreters to ensure they will be able to clearly hear the speakers, as well as have enough working space, particularly a surface to support their notepad, documents, and a microphone. If they are working in a meeting room, they should sit at the table together with the speakers, but in a conference hall, if there is a special podium for the speaker, the interpreter should ask the organisers to arrange a second podium or a table and chair set up for their use, because

> "[i]t can be a rather harrowing experience trying to support one's notepad with one hand while taking notes with the other while at the same time juggling a handheld microphone on stage in front of hundreds of people, especially when doing long consecutive on a difficult speech" (ibidem).

Whether simultaneous or consecutive interpreting, the crucial factor determining the success or otherwise of communication is congruence, which is defined as "the degree to which verbal and nonverbal communication correspond with or contradict one another" (Eunson 2008, 257). People, in general, tend to subconsciously trust those who exbibit body language that is congruent with their verbal messages and mistrust those whose non-verbal signals contradict their verbally expressed message. Hence, it is vital for the interpreter not to leave their body language to chance but to match it to the speaker's verbal message, with the intention of producing a better communicative impression. At the end of the day, this is precisely the main purpose of every single interpretation task – rendering the message into the target language in such a way so that it produces the same (or as similar as possible) effect on the audience as the speaker had intended.

When discussing body language and non-verbal communication, there is yet another related aspect worth mentioning, and one that may significantly improve or undermine the interpreter's performance, i. e. the interpreter's own posture. As observed by (Marković 2017, 22), standing in the background (as in the consecutive mode) or being invisible for the audience (as in the simultaneous mode), may give the interpreters a sense of comfort and anonymity, encouraging them to adopt a relaxed body posture. Most of the time, they do not even realize that since they are too busy processing and producing the information. Nevertheless, numerous studies[50] have proved that the posture and body movement affect one's physiology and offer certain psychological benefits.

Amy Cuddy, a Harvard social psychologist, in her famous 2012 TED talk named "Your body language may shape who you are"[51] discusses the effects that

---

50 See, for instance: Carney, Cuddy, Yap 2010; Hassmen, Koivula, Uutela 2000; Peper & Lin 2012.
51 https://www.youtube.com/watch?v=Ks-_Mh1QhMc, accessed 11.03.2023.

one's posture and gestures have on the hormonal levels and the feeling of power. In her talk, she mentions the so-called "power poses", i.e. poses characterized by expansive positions, erect posture, and open limbs, and she claims that they cause neuroendocrine and behavioural changes in a person, particularly in terms of their testosterone and cortisol levels. A high power pose means positioning one's body in a way that takes up more space and the limbs are arranged more openly, whereas a low power pose is exactly the opposite. In the experiment, those participants who used high power poses "[...] experienced elevations in testosterone, decreases in cortisol, and increased feelings of power and tolerance for risk; low-power posers exhibited the opposite pattern" (Carney et al. 2010).[52] Judging by those results, one may assume that if the simultaneous interpreters, performing their job in a booth, adopt a low power pose (for instance, closing their limbs, rounding their shoulders, and slouching their back – all of which is very likely, considering the limited amount of space at their disposal), their testosterone levels may drop and they might experience a feeling of powerlessness, which may significantly affect their self-esteem, self-confidence and, as a result, their entire performance. Such a position signals uncertainty, weakness, doubt, and negative feelings (Marković 2017, 28). On the other hand, sitting in an erect position, even for a short time, would produce "changes in your hormones, energy levels, strength, and moods" (Peper et al. 2016, 70). Those who sit in an erect position also have better mood, feel more confident, and appear more trustworthy (Marković 2017, 28).

It is not only posture that has an impact on the interpreter's job. Two researchers from the University of Kansas, Kraft and Pressman (2012), studied the influence of smiling on stress recovery. In the experiment they conducted they subjected the participants to certain multitasking-requiring activities (all of which were also stress-inducing). Those subjects who were instructed to smile proved to have lower heart rate levels after recovering from these activities. Therefore, the researchers concluded that adopting positive facial expressions, such as a smile, when performing stressful activities, may provide both physiological and psychological benefits (Kraft and Pressman 2012, 1372). These findings may prove particularly useful for interpreters who, by the very nature of their job, are constantly engaged in multitasking activities and experience high levels of stress. If an interpreter learns to smile during his/her interpreting task, they may have a lower heart rate and recover more quickly from stress.

Although some may still argue that the job of an interpreter revolves, first and foremost, around the verbal content expressed by the speaker, it cannot be denied that the awareness, proper recognition and rendition of the non-verbal elements, may play an equally crucial role and may largely determine the success

---

52 https://pubmed.ncbi.nlm.nih.gov/20855902/, accessed 11.03.2023.

of otherwise of the entire interpretation task. Hence, an interpreter should never stop developing their perception of non-verbal language, as well as their own non-verbal skills. As noticed by Marković (2017, 23), "the goal of the interpreter is to strive for ever increasing excellence, both as a listener and a speaker". Viaggio (1997, 291) expresses a similar opinion, though in a more poetic manner:

> "It is up to trainers, then, to teach would-be practitioners to listen with their eyes and speak with their bodies, and fully to incorporate paralanguage and kinesics as a crucial part of their own message, since both are an inalienable part of a speaker's 'articulateness', and that is precisely what the interpreter is: a *sui generis* speaker".

To sum all that has been said so far about the non-verbal communication in the interpreting context, it is an inseparable element of any interpreter's job and involves multiple elements related to the way one speaks, dresses, positions oneself and moves. It is not only the speaker who conveys messages and emotions via body language, but also the interpreter, whose body movements and voice modulation may render the speaker's intended message. Also, the interpreter's body posture and movement has a significant effect on their physiology, mood, as well as stress levels. Therefore, in their job the interpreters do not render just the verbal message expressed by the speaker, but also communicate their own moods, attitudes, and feelings. Awareness of non-verbal signals helps interpreters to better understand the speaker's intention, to influence their body physiology, and to produce or highlight meaning with their own movement. Thus, awareness of the speaker's as well as one's own body language may make interpreters better communicators overall.

Nevertheless, sometimes no matter how professional, competent, well-prepared and aware of non-verbal cues the interpreter is, and no matter how well the interpretation setting is arranged, some problems are simply bound to occur and certain errors will inevitably appear. These will constitute the topic of the next subchapter.

4.3   Errors in Interpreting

Errors in interpreting are understood as any deviations from the original text (Tryuk 2007, 110). Barik (1975/2002, after Tryuk 2007, 110–111) classified these errors into the following three categories:

1. Omissions:
   - omitting one lexical element, for instance an adjective or an adverb;
   - omitting a larger text fragment as a result of failure to understand it;
   - linking fragments of sentences together while at the same time omitting other fragments.

2. Additions:
   - adding an attributive, for example: ...*they both had <u>deeply</u> rooted within themselves...*
   - making the target text more complex than the original one, for instance: *I must be aware and <u>conscious</u> of what is just and <u>fair</u>...*
   - adding a linking element which is absent in the original and changes the logical organization of the text, for example: *I also enjoyed very much the performance of the actors <u>because</u> the two starts were...*
   - adding a conclusion despite its absence in the original text, for instance: *... men who decide the selection of the books which are going to be published and how they are going to be offered <u>to the public</u>...*
3. Substitutions (errors resulting in semantic changes).

Kopczyński (1980, after Tryuk 2007, 111–112) provided another classification of errors:
1. Translation errors (for instance, lack of equivalence).
2. Errors of linguistic competence (for example lexical and syntactic errors).
3. Performance errors (such as hesitation, stammering, repetitions, false starts, omissions and additions).

These errors indicate that the interpreter has not yet mastered the two important interpreting strategies, that is planning one's speech and controlling one's own language production.

As regards consecutive interpreting specifically, the following classification of errors was proposed (Gonzales 1996, Barik 1998, Hairuo 2015, after Malau et al. 2021, 73–74):
1. Literal translation – in which the interpreter focuses solely on substituting words from one language to another.
2. Inadequate language proficiency – the interpreter is unable to anticipate language patterns in sentences and expressions. This may lead to two types of error: a lexical error which is the distortion and misunderstanding of the words' meaning; and incorrect translation whereby the interpreter is unable to transfer the message from the source to the target language.
3. Failure to preserve the register (i. e. the formality level of the original speech).
4. Distortion – which results in losing the original meaning, usually due to deficient language skills, memory problems or insufficient interpretation skills.
5. Omission – the interpreter deletes some information expressed in the source language speech, it may take one of the following forms (Barik 1971):
   - skipping omission – the interpreter deletes a word or a short phrase;

- comprehension omission – the interpreter is unable to understand some parts in the text, which leads to the loss in meaning;
- compounding omission – the interpreter joins two sentences together and deletes some phrases.

6. Addition – the interpreter adds some information when rendering the speech. Types of additions, as distinguished by Barik (1971), have already been discussed at the beginning of this subchapter.

7. Failure to preserve the paralinguistic features – this may take the following forms:
   - fillers – the interpreter makes pauses and produces sounds such as "euu, hm";
   - incomplete sentences – they are produced when the interpreter is feeling under considerable pressure and experiences major difficulties in expressing ideas;
   - repeated words or phrases – the interpreter repeats certain words or expressions, which, in turn, may affect speech fluency.

Regardless of the nature of errors that may occur during interpreting, every single one of them may affect the overall assessment of the interpreter's performance and this very assessment is going to be the topic of the following subchapter.

4.4   Interpreting Assessment

For years, the assessment of conference interpreting has been focused mainly on three predominant issues: interpreting assessment in terms of the faithfulness to the source text or loyalty towards its author; evaluation of the comprehensibility of the target text and its accuracy in terms of transferring the source text information and message, and the accuracy of its linguistic form, i.e. lexis, terminology, phraseology, as well as syntactic, stylistic, semantic and pragmatic accuracy (Tryuk 2007, 134). Some additional elements considered in interpretation assessment are the aesthetics of the interpretation, which entails not only the linguistic means selected and the interpreter's fluency, but it also concerns the sound of the interpreter's voice, and his/her improvement of the quality of the target text, following the listeners' expectations. According to Déjean Le Féal (1991, after Tryuk 2007, 134), if the recipients of conference interpretation praise the interpreter saying that his/her interpretation was better than the original speech, it by no means should be perceived as an insult. On the contrary, this is an obvious compliment.

In Poland, some of the most significant studies on the evaluation of conference interpreting, the interpreter's behaviour, as well as the listeners' expectations, was carried out by Kopczyński (1994). He evaluated interpretation quality in terms of two dimensions: the linguistic and the pragmatic one. The former entails that the interpretation adheres to the linguistic norms, whereas the latter is related with the following:
– the speaker, his/her status and the status of the message recipients;
– the speaker's intention;
– the speaker's attitude towards the message and the message recipients;
– the recipients' attitude towards the speaker and his/her message;
– the interpreter, his/her interpreting competence, behaviour and interpreting strategies;
– the form of the message;
– the illocutionary[53] strength of the message;
– interactional and interpretation norms in a given linguistic community;
– the place (Kopczyński 1994, after Tryuk 2007, 137–138).

Kopczyński (1994) studied three main groups of recipients participating in international conferences as either speakers or delegates, i.e. the humanists (philologists, historians, lawyers, economists), representatives of exact sciences (for instance, engineers and doctors), as well as diplomats. The researcher focused on the assessment of the following parameters:
– transferring the general message of the source language speech;
– transferring the complete message of the source language speech;
– terminological precision;
– style;
– grammatical accuracy;
– fluency of interpretation;
– diction;
– voice quality (Kopczyński 1994, after Tryuk 2007, 138).

The research proved that what both the speakers and the listeners valued most was the interpreter's ability to transfer the entire message, with the terminological precision and the form coming right after. For speakers themselves, the interpreter's fluency was of utmost importance. For humanists the crucial factors were: the full transfer of the original content, terminology and grammatical accuracy; the scientists and diplomats valued the two aspects that the humanists

---

53 Illocution is understood as "an act of speaking or writing which in itself effects or constitutes the intended action, e.g. ordering, warning, or promising" (https://languages.oup.com/goo gle-dictionary-en/, accessed 15.03.2023).

did, i.e. the full transfer of the original content, and terminology, but they also considered fluency to be very important.

In the same research Kopczyński (1994, after Tryuk 2007, 138–139) also studied the listener's tolerance to certain mistakes and errors made by interpreters:
- inadequate terminology;
- ungrammatical sentences;
- stylistic mistakes;
- unfinished sentences;
- lack of fluency;
- bad diction;
- monotonous intonation;
- uneven rhythm;
- too general conveyance of the content;
- too detailed conveyance of the content.

According to the research results, what the speakers found most annoying were: inadequate terminology and too general conveyance of the original message, whereas the listeners found unfinished and ungrammatical sentences to be the most disturbing. Humanists complained most about inadequate terminology and unfinished sentences; the scientists – about inadequate terminology and ungrammatical sentences, whereas the diplomats – about inadequate terminology and an uneven rhythm.

The study was concluded with the opinions expressed by all the participant groups about the role of an interpreter and proved that the respondents were almost unanimous. They all expressed the view that the interpreter should have empathy which means that he/she should be able to convey the speaker's intentions, as well as his/her non-verbal and paraverbal behaviour. As regards the interpretation itself, the crucial aspect was the content and not the form, followed by terminological accuracy (Kopczyński 1994, after Tryuk 2007, 139).

Another study, conducted by Collados Aís (1998/2002, after Tryuk 2007, 139), proved that the monotonous intonation of an interpreter has a negative impact on the listeners' perception and their assessment of the interpreting. In this particular study, the interpreter's monotonous intonation was evaluated negatively, whereas a more dynamic intonation – positively. Curiously enough, the study participants failed to pay attention to semantic mistakes which were deliberately introduced into this more dynamic interpretation. Monotony may also affect the perception of other factors affecting the quality of interpreting, such as: a native accent, how pleasant the voice seems to the listeners, fluency, logical coherence, accurate terminology, style and diction.

Hence, the study proved that there is a significant difference between the interpreting quality and its perception; it is the latter that largely determines the interpreter's success or otherwise. On the basis of the study quoted, Tryuk (2007, 140) concludes that the quality criteria change according to the interpretation recipients and hence the conference participants should be viewed as crucial here. She also observes that the study of the interpretation quality, as perceived by monolingual recipients, does not seem to be objective because, according to Ackermann (1998, 168, after Tryuk 2007, 140), interpretation quality is a sum of subjectively-perceived components such as: faithfulness of the target text in relation to the source text, the interpreter's linguistic skills, his/her voice, prosodic features (such as pitch, stress, segment length, tone and intonation), diction, the knowledge of specialist terms. All these elements are assessed individually and subjectively.

One of the most important aspects is if the interpreter managed to understand the text's meaning and the speaker's intentions and if, on the basis of these, he/she is capable of formulating a correct text that the listeners would understand. However, the interpreter is frequently under time pressure, which forces him/her to selectively process the source text and rendering into the target language only the information that he/she deems crucial. And this is something that a monolingual listener is unable to verify, therefore, interpreting quality assessment is largely affected by the inability to check exactly the extent to which the target text is faithful to the original one. As long as the target language speech is coherent, the recipients are unlikely to notice that the interpreter added, omitted or changed something. Sometimes this coherence may successfully conceal the fact that the interpreter had significant problems comprehending the source text and introduced changes to the target version. On the other hand, an interpreter who tries to convey all the source information, but does this in an incoherent and influent manner, may be severely criticized by the listeners. However, this may not be the fault of the interpreter, but rather of the poor coherence of the source text – nevertheless, the interpreter will be to blame in such a situation and his/her interpreting assessment will be rather low (Tryuk 2007, 140–141). Also, it seems that interpreters who speak with energy and modulate their voice are rated much higher that those who speak in a monotonous voice, regardless of the accuracy of their interpretation and of how much of the original information they manage to convey faithfully. What tends to be mainly remembered by the listeners is the general impression of the interpreter's performance, instead of errors or inconsistencies in relation to the original text. Besides, the recipients do not tend to pay attention to individual terminological errors as long their specialist knowledge allows them to complete the missing information pieces or rectify the incorrect ones, as well as clarify the issues which seem unclear in the source text (Tryuk 2007, 141).

According to Riccardi (2002, 116), the main criterion for assessing the interpreting quality is the interpreter's impact on the listeners. The listeners are rarely able to notice the differences between the source and the target texts. However, what they do notice are illogical and nonsensical statements, unfinished sentences, errors in specialist terminology. If these do not occur, no one tends to criticize the interpreter. Therefore, as regards the interpretation that is faithful, equivalent and accurate in terms of the register and style, the interpreter is only responsible to oneself (Tryuk 2007, 141). Although the interpreter and his/her performance may be evaluated by a fellow colleague, such evaluations are rarely disclosed to the general public for fear of disturbing the atmosphere among interpreters who have to cooperate with each other. Hence, every single interpreter is responsible for his/her self-evaluation and acting as one's own critic (Tryuk 2007, 142).

In the process of training conference interpreters, what tends to be continually assessed is the interpreter's mastery of certain *know-how* which encompasses the following: linguistic accuracy, avoiding interference, applying various problem-solving strategies (e.g. using paraphrases), as well as the cognitive component entailing the ability to mentally process and coordinate efforts necessary for this entire complex operation (Gile 1995, after Tryuk 2007, 143). What is also involved is the methodological-strategic component which means the mastery of techniques and strategies used in conference interpreting (e.g. the note-taking technique for consecutive interpreting), as well as being faithful to the original message and comprehensible to the listeners, while transmitting the maximum of the source text information.

Although, as already mentioned, the individual criteria for assessing the quality of interpreting may vary according to the situation as well as the audience, the official website of the European Union provides the following ones for assessing the quality of consecutive and simultaneous interpreting, respectively:

Marking criteria for consecutive interpreting

Content	
– Coherence/ plausibility – Completeness/ Accuracy – Knowledge of passive language?	– Was the logic of the original speech clearly recognizable? – Was the message coherent? – Were the main ideas and the structure rendered? – Were there any significant omissions with an impact on the coherence of the speech? – Were there any important mistakes ("contresens")? – Did the interpretation render the original ideas/information of the speech accurately? – Was the content conveyed in full? – Were there too many details missing? – Were there any misleading or redundant additions ("embroidery")? – Overuse of redundant filler phrases?

Delivery/Form – Quality of active language – Communication skills	– Knowledge of target language (correct grammar, appropriate register, idiomatic expressions, vocabulary, interferences from the source language)? – Appropriate choice of register? – Terminology? – Diction (mumbling or clear enunciation)? – Accent (if applicable)? – Pace of delivery (fluent or staccato)? – Use of the voice (prosody)? Intonation? – Was the delivery professional? Was it agreeable to listen to and confident? – Eye contact? – Appropriate body language?
Technique – Interpretation strategies	– Literal rendition of speech or intelligent processing of content? – Use of interpretation strategies (paraphrasing, output monitoring, ability to condense information, "telescoping")? – Ability to monitor output? – Note-taking technique? – Time of delivery (shorter/longer than original speech)? Was the overrun excessive? – Finishing sentences

Table 8. Marking criteria for consecutive interpreting (source: https://europa.eu/interpretation/doc/marking_criteria_en.pdf, accessed 15.03.2023).

Marking criteria for simultaneous interpreting

Content – Coherence/ plausibility – Completeness/ Accuracy – Knowledge of passive language?	– Was the logic of the original speech clearly recognizable? – Was the message coherent? – Were the main ideas and the structure rendered? – Were there any significant omissions with an impact on the coherence of the speech? – Were there any important mistakes ("contresens")? – Did the interpretation render the original ideas/information of the speech accurately? – Was the content conveyed in full? – Were there too many details missing? – Were there any misleading or redundant additions ("embroidery")? – Overuse of redundant filler phrases?

Delivery/Form – Quality of active language – Communication skills	– Knowledge of target language (correct grammar, appropriate register, idiomatic expressions, vocabulary, interferences from the source language)? – Appropriate choice of register? – Terminology? – Diction (mumbling or clear enunciation)? – Accent (if applicable)? – Pace of delivery (fluent or staccato)? – Use of the voice (prosody)? Intonation? – Was the delivery professional? Was it agreeable to listen to and confident? – Fluency of the delivery ("décalage")? No abrupt or lengthy hesitations)? – Stamina? – Microphone discipline?
Technique – Interpretation strategies	– Literal rendition of speech or intelligent processing of content? – Use of interpretation strategies (paraphrasing, output monitoring, ability to condense information, "telescoping")? – Ability to monitor output? – Finishing sentences?

Table 9. Marking criteria for simultaneous interpreting (source: https://europa.eu/interpre tation/doc/marking_criteria_en.pdf, accessed 15.03.2023).

In assessment of the quality of interpreting, whether for trainee or professional interpreters, one may use questionnaires, surveys, evaluation reports, etc. For instance, in an evaluation questionnaire used at the University of Trieste, the following criteria are being assessed:
– equivalence between the source and the target text (which entails that both texts convey the same message, preserve the same communicate function, as well as produce a similar effect on the recipients);
– precision (which means that the information expressed in the source text is conveyed precisely in the target text, taking into consideration such parameters as: pragmatic dimension, information relevance to the listeners, specialist knowledge of both the speaker and the listeners, the speaker's intention);
– appropriateness (adjusting the target text culturally, stylistically and in terms of the register, to the listener's expectations, as well as to the situation in which it has been formulated; appropriateness may be achieved by modifying and adapting the source text to the target culture both stylistically and rhetorically);
– interpretation's usefulness (this means formulating a target text that would be clear, comprehensible and possible to be used by the recipients in a certain context and situation (Riccardi 2002, after Tryuk 2007, 146).

Evaluation of interpretation quality may be done from different perspectives: one may assess equivalence and precision of the target text in relation to the source text; one may analyze the target text and its function in the given communicative situation via evaluation of its appropriateness and usefulness; or one may study the target text's usefulness as an autonomous text. The evaluation form for consecutive and simultaneous interpreting, applied by Riccardi (2002), involves the previously mentioned macrocriteria (i. e. equivalence, precision, appropriateness and usefulness), together with microcriteria which concern such parameters as: phonological, prosodic and lexical accuracy (including terminological accuracy), morphosyntactic and semantic accuracy, defects in production (such as pauses, self-corrections, unfinished sentences), additions, omissions, register, technique, gesticulation, eye contact, etc. General interpretation quality is determined by the success in conveying the source information in the target language. On the other hand, in the formative assessment, both the macro and microcriteria are taken into consideration. For instance, The equivalence parameter is evaluated by the number of logical and semantic errors that occur, as well as the number of omissions and additions. The precision criterion is related to the quality of the lexical, morphosyntactic and prosodic dimensions. Appropriateness is ensured, for instance, by the correct selection of the register; and usefulness – by the prosodic, phonological and lexical accuracy (Tryuk 2007, 147).

All (or at least some) of the aforementioned criteria for assessing the interpretation, may be applied to evaluate the interpreting performance, whether of a novice or a professional interpreter. However, although numerous and varied, they all fail to account for the fact that interpreting can be considered a creative process, and from this very perspective interpreting will be presented in the following chapter.

Chapter 5:
Creativity in Interpreting

5.1 What is Creativity?

Creativity is a complex and multifaceted notion which can be defined in various ways depending on the perspective that one takes. One of the most common views is that creativity is connected with genius and in this view the ruling criterion for creativity is uniqueness (Horváth 2012, 123). When trying to define a genius, Eysenck (1995, 124) states that it depends on the coincidence of certain personality variables, as well as particular social conditions. Apart from such components as intelligence and talent, the scholar enumerates other conditions affecting a genius, such as: socioeconomic status, gender, religion, home environment, intellectual stimulation, age, lifespan, motivation, and even the season of birth (1995, 124–169).

An interesting view on creativity is presented by Gruber and Davis (1988), who claim that creativity, contrary to what people tend to think when admiring the works of creative individuals, is not a sudden burst of enlightenment, but rather a slowly evolving process of reflection and discovery.

Yet another approach to creativity is one that, instead of focusing on the works and achievements of creative people, stresses individual differences in creativity and the correlations between them. According to this approach, creativity is viewed as an innate personality trait which means that every single person is considered creative, and the products of creativity are not necessarily works or discoveries, but they encompass a wide range of outputs including behaviours, performances, ideas, things (Taylor 1988, 104). Creative products may also include scientific theories, jokes, advertising campaigns, and many other (Perkins 1988, 378).

Torrance (1988, 66–67) enumerates the following characteristic features of creative thinking: flexibility; originality, unusualness, or rarity of the response; elaboration; emotional expressiveness; synthesis or combination; unusual visualization; internal visualization; humour.

He also stresses the importance of personal involvement, saying that creative people need to love what they do and this, in turn, allows them to develop other personality traits that are characteristic of a creative person, such as courage, independent thinking, good judgement, honesty, perseverance, curiosity, willingness to take risks (1988, 68).

As regards the creative process itself, Wallas identified four stages:
- preparation, in which one feels the need for a solution or perceives some deficiency; at this stage one clarifies the problem and engages in random exploration;
- incubation, during which one reads, discusses, explores and formulates a range of possible solutions, which are then critically analyzed in terms of their possible benefits and drawbacks;
- illumination, in which one comes up with a new solution or idea;
- revision, where one experiments with the solution or idea in order to evaluate and perfect it (Torrance 1988, 44).

Yet another view on creativity takes into account the cognitive perspective and according to this approach, creative thinking entails the ability to connect things and ideas that have not been connected before. While analytical thinking is logical, predictable and convergent (i. e. governed by rules and aimed at finding a single solution), creative thinking requires imagination and leads to several solutions. Both analytical and creative thinking are useful and needed in everyday life (Szabó 2002, 83–85).

There is also an adaptational view of creativity, whereby creativity is perceived as the ability to adapt to new situations, environments and circumstances. Representatives of this view, such as Komlósi (1987), Schank (1988) and Barron (1988), claim that creativity is the ability to respond flexibly and adaptively to the needs for new approaches and new products.

In her research on creativity, Komlósi concluded that not only is it an adaptational process, but, when found themselves in challenging conditions, creative people are more open to stimuli and able to better, more quickly and accurately recognize neutral stimuli than the non-creative individuals (Komlósi 1987, 19). The results of her research appear to be consistent with the findings of Kovács (1987) who also studied creativity and claims that creative people have an open and flexible attitude and are always ready to change their perspective of viewing things; they also tend to process information faster, as well as are able to use information in elementary processes (Kovács 1987, 49).

According to yet another approach to creativity, it is inextricably linked to problem-solving, understood as an ability to use specific procedures, techniques and operations in order to accomplish a given goal, and it requires the formation and application of novel strategies. In order to solve a certain problem, a person needs to use the information they have, which, when coupled with their former experiences, together form new structures enabling them to solve this particular problem (Landau 1976, 25, 76). In problem-solving, similarly as in decision-making, the following three abilities are indispensable: analysis (breaking down a complex whole into smaller parts), synthesis (putting the parts together to form a larger whole), and evaluation (assessing it in terms of values and norms) (Szabó 2002, 14).

As illustrated by the above description of the problem-solving process, it emphasizes the role of former knowledge and experiences and these play an equally significant role in creativity. Some scholars (such as Sternberg 1988, or Weisberg 1988) stress the significance of prior knowledge and experiences in one's ability to handle novelty, claiming that is would not be possible to come up with new ideas about something, without knowing anything about it (Sternberg 1988, 137), or without having a knowledge of the domain in question (Weisberg 1988, 155).

Studies have also proved that there is a correlation between creativity and tolerance of frustration. For instance, Kakas (1987) asserts that creative individuals have certain personality traits that may help them lower the level of frustration in difficult situations. Interestingly enough, she claims that a creativity-requiring task, i. e. one that needs an individual to do more than just automatically implement his/her knowledge, itself constitutes a source of frustration (Kakas 1987, 79). Hence, it follows that less creative people are less able to solve a problem in a frustrating situation and they are more likely to give in to the feeling of frustration and anger, as well as experience an emotional block.

As already mentioned at the beginning of this chapter, creativity is a very complex construct and its definition and understanding is determined by the perspective one adopts and examines it from. Nevertheless, one may say that creativity is no longer considered to be a privilege of the lucky few, but rather a personality or a cognitive trait that is shared by all people, though the degree to which it manifests itself varies from person to person. Personality traits typically ascribed to creative individuals include flexibility, originality, independence and perseverance, but the realization of one's creative potential is determined by a range of factors, including prior knowledge, motivation, environment and personal experiences.

One may claim that the above-mentioned creativity-related traits are also ones expected from a professional interpreter, and indeed, interpreting may be perceived as a creative process, and as such will be presented and discussed in the following subchapter.

5.2   Interpreting as a Creative Process

Creativity in interpreting can be studied in terms of three predominant aspects, i. e.: the products, the mental processes, and the interpreter's behaviour. The first aspect mentioned views interpreting from the perspective of the product, whereas the remaining ones perceive it from the point of view of the process (Horváth 2012, 134). All these perspectives will be discussed in the subchapters that follow.

5.2.1   Creative Products in Interpreting

Although when thinking about creativity in translation, one tends to have written translation in mind, a lot of creative aspects can be applied to interpreting as well, despite the obvious differences between these two types in terms of the mode, time pressure, stress level, etc. However, according to the results of a survey conducted by Horváth (2010) among the interpreters, the respondents frequently failed to perceive interpreting as a creative activity since the original message was created by someone other than the interpreter him/herself. Hence, it appears that a lot of interpreters, when deciding if a certain activity is creative or not, tend to assume that in order for it to be deemed creative, something unique needs to be produced and only few people are able to do this. However, Horváth (2012, 134) argues that this is a myth and she seems to be right in claiming so, particularly when considering the definitions of creativity discussed in the previous section, which stated that creativity involves a wide range of different outputs, including behaviours, performances, ideas, etc. Such a view on creativity is also one that will be adopted throughout this book.

As already mentioned, creativity tends to be associated with written translation in general, and literary translation in particular. Non-literary texts are relatively rarely considered creative since they tend to be viewed as mostly informative and containing very little or no originality. However, Cho (2006, 380) claims that all texts are original, but the degree of this originality varies from text to text. Therefore, the translators of non-literary texts need to be just as creative when performing their tasks as literary translators, but the nature of this creativity will obviously be quite different due to the different nature of the texts they are faced with (Pagnoulle 1993, 89). Since interpreters deal predominantly with non-literary texts, one may assume that they will also be expected to display creativity, similarly to that which is required from non-literary translators.

Both translation and interpreting can be considered "recreation" (Kussmaul 1995) because, rather than rendering the source text into the target language in an automatic, mechanical way, they entail that the translator or the interpreter creates a text that would be equivalent to the source one, but would also differ from it in many respects and involve new elements, non-existent in the original text. Hence, creativity here is linked to this new nature of the final product (Kussmaul 1995, 121). A similar opinion is expressed by Horváth (2012, 136) who states that "[...] the translator/interpreter is not simply 'parroting' the target language text but contributes actively to the creation of the target-language message". Cho (2006, 381) points out that creativity is necessary in order to eliminate the linguistic or textual interference[54] caused by the source language or the source text. Nevertheless, she also observed that the level of creativity may vary according to the language pair, and when the two languages in question are significantly different because, for instance, they belong to two distant language families, then the translator's or the interpreter's creativity might be hindered (2006, 378).

Pagnoulle, who studied creativity in non-literary translation, observed that when the source text is poorly organized or incorrect in some respects, the translator needs to do much more than simply translate it; he/she is then allowed to introduce certain changes to it or reformulate it. As a result, the entire process can be called an "adaptation" rather than "translation" (Pagnoulle 1993, 79). It seems that the same principle is applicable to the process of interpreting as well.

The scholars mentioned above are not the only ones who claim that translation/interpreting is a creative activity. For instance, MacRae (1989) argues that, as regards interpreting, creativity is not solely linked to the formulation of the source language message in the target language. In her view, the interpreter may exhibit their creativity, for example, in their task preparation, note-taking techniques, their interpreting style and the awareness and avoidance of the possible traps. These may entail, for instance, using the techniques of skimming and scanning the materials when preparing for the interpreting event, focusing on charts and diagrams, preparing terminology lists, making glossaries, etc. MacRae states that creativity in interpreting is inextricably linked to the development of one's own unique interpreting style and one's own techniques for analyzing and processing information in order to best fulfil the interpreting purpose. To illustrate this, she provides an example of the interpreter finding a way to continue speaking without unnecessary breaks, and without waiting for the verb to come, when translating between V/O languages (such as English,

---

54 The term interference (Polish: "interferencja") is defined by Tomaszkiewicz (2006, 44) as: "Błąd tłumaczeniowy wynikający z niewiedzy lub ze złej techniki przekładowej, polegający na zastosowaniu w tekście docelowym formy językowej charakterystycznej dla języka wyjściowego". ("Translation error resulting from lack of knowledge or inadequate translation technique, and consisting in using in the target text a linguistic form that is typical of the source language"). (Author's own translation).

Spanish) and O/V languages (such as German, Japanese) (MacRae 1989, 152–153).

Another situation in which the interpreter's creativity may be manifested is when the speaker uses neologisms, which may be defined as "[...] newly coined lexical units or existing lexical units that acquire a new sense" (Newmark 1988, 140). As regards neologisms in interpreting situations, Niska (1998, 12) differentiates between two types: the source language terms and speaker-specific phrases and expressions; and the possible neologisms that the interpreter uses to translate either these source language terms or speaker-specific expressions, or other terms and expressions which lack direct equivalents in the target language. As for the expressions specific to the speaker, they are frequently spontaneous, idiosyncratic and coined on the spot, thus being the products of the speaker's creativity. Hence, the interpreter also needs to render them on the spot and therefore the end result of such an interpretation may be considered the product of the interpreter's creativity (Horváth 2012, 138).

All the creative products discussed above are certainly results of the two extremely important processes involved in interpreting, i. e. problem-solving and decision-making. These two can also be considered elements of the interpreter's creativity – specifically, the interpreter's creative mental processes – and hence the following subchapter is going to have a closer look at them.

5.2.2 Creative Mental Processes in Interpreting: Problem-solving and Decision-making

A translator or an interpreter may be perceived as a language mediator whose competence entails much more than merely the knowledge of the languages in question. Due to the specific nature of their job, they are also required to have an extralinguistic knowledge, multiple language skills and intelligence, as well as creativity and the ability to identify and then solve a plethora of translation or interpretation problems (Walter 1988, 108). For Walter (ibidem), creativity is very closely linked to the ability to search for and find solutions to translation/interpretation problems. When talking about the translator's/interpreter's process of selection of equivalents, she distinguished between controlled and uncontrolled activities. In her understanding, the controlled ones refer to the automatically selected "one-to-one" equivalents, whereas the uncontrolled selection tends to be quite unpredictable and requiring more creativity from the translator/interpreter. The scholar states that "controlled decisions occur most frequently in the translation of highly standardized texts under standardized communicative conditions" (1988, 108).

However, as observed by Horváth (2012, 140), as regards the interpreting process, one needs to distinguish between two kinds of smaller processes within it, i. e. a longer one which includes the stage of the very preparation for the task and the event, then performing the task and evaluating it after it has ended; and a shorter process of the actual interpreting act. As stated by Horváth (ibidem), during the interpreting process "[…] a lot of factors, linguistic and extra-linguistic, come into play simultaneously under very stringent time constraints". Hence, the role of the interpreter's creativity cannot be underestimated. A similar view is expressed by Wills (1996), according to whom this dynamic aspect of the interpreter's creativity manifests itself not only in the formulation of the source language message, but also in the simultaneous confrontation with the source text and the target code, as well as in decoding and encoding strategies (Wilss 1996, 166).

The interpreting process can be considered a creative activity not only because of the decoding and encoding strategies, as mentioned by Wills (ibidem), but also because it may be regarded as a problem-solving activity with the source text being the problem and the target text – the solution. Using the limited set of cues or gradually incoming elements, within the spans of merely a few seconds, the interpreter has to arrive at a correct conclusion or be capable of predicting both the message and the incoming elements in such a way that he/she can organize his target language rendition accordingly. During this entire process, he/she, rather than merely repeating something uttered by somebody else, but in another language, is truly engaging in a creative process (Riccardi 1998, 172). Riccardi (ibidem) stresses the importance of something that has already been discussed in subchapter 2.2.2, namely: anticipation, which entails figuring out how to close down an open meaning even before the closing elements actually appear. This implies that the interpreter needs to, first of all, depend on what has already been said and done in a given communicative situation, and, at the same time, use his/her creative imagination to try and foresee what is going to be said next. And, as rightly observed by Horváth (2012, 141), "[i]t requires from the interpreter not only resourcefulness and ingenuity but also a certain amount of empathy, a quality closely related to creativity".

What was also mentioned by Riccardi was the importance of coming to a right conclusion during the interpreting process, which necessitates both divergent and convergent thinking. The former involves searching for alternatives in order to find several equally viable solutions to a problem which, in the interpreter's case, would be a range of possible linguistic solutions to an open problem as the source language message is still unfolding, in order to come up with the best possible equivalent of the source text message. Then, the process of selecting only one among the several target language alternatives necessitates convergent thinking, which is used to narrow down exploration, but, at the same time, is a process generally perceived as less creative. Nevertheless, being able to select between these two modes of thinking can also be considered a proof of creativity (Gabora 2002, after Horváth 2012, 141). This particular strategy, when employed by interpreters, enables them to avoid commitment to a single solution and to see the bigger picture of the possible linguistic solutions.

When discussing creative mental processes of an interpreter, MacRae (1989) lists the following: abstracting, directed remembering, imagination/invention, and association. However, she states that these strategies are by no means "all inclusive" (MacRae 1989, 150). Imagination/invention are mental processes that make the entire interpreting process original and the imaginative feature of an interpretation manifests itself in the interpreter's selection of words and images. She observes that the ultimate test of an interpreter's imagination and inventiveness is his/her ability to render a joke from one language or cultural context to another (ibidem). As regards the next mental process, i.e. association, MacRae states that an experienced interpreter, when allowing their mind to wander freely in the background of the interpreting process, is still able to make associations (or connections) between statements made at different times by the same speaker, or by different speakers, which, in turn, enables the interpreter to suddenly grasp a concept, or relate some statement that has been uttered, to something that has been mentioned previously, or to something that the interpreter happens to know from his/her previous experience (MacRae 1989, 151–152).

Nevertheless, as stated by Horváth (2012, 143), an interpreter who is performing his/her interpreting task, does not really have the time for lengthy analyses, which, in turn, presupposes a great amount of spontaneity, flexibility, fluency and originality on his/her part, all of which, as illustrated in the previous subchapters, are closely related to creativity.

However, the interpreter's creativity involves not only certain products and processes, as demonstrated in the subchapters above, but also particular behaviours, and these are going to be elaborated on in the following section.

5.2.3 Creative Behaviour in Interpreting

In order to study the interpreter's creative behaviour, it is necessary to analyze the interpreting process, as well as the communicative situation in which it takes place. One may distinguish two main views here: the strategies-view, which concentrates on the cognitive aspects; and the situational view, which adopts a wider perspective, focusing also on the global context, the time frame and the participants in the communicative act (Horváth 2012, 145). However, when discussing creativity in translation, Cho observes that creativity is not necessary in all stages of translation since a lot of the translation process in time tends to become automatic, depending on the translator's familiarity with the subject matter in question, experience and language skills (Cho 2006, 380). Nevertheless, Horváth (ibidem) disagrees with this view saying that although certain mental processes involved in translation (or interpretation) become automatic over time, the situation always changes and hence every single assignment displays different characteristics in terms of place, participants, subject matter, issues to be discussed, etc., all of which, as she claims, requires the interpreter to use his/her creativity. She further supports this claim with the view expressed by Torrance (1988, 47) who stated that in the interpretation process the interpreter needs to respond constructively to the novel situations, rather than merely adapting to them. This constructive response entails the interpreter's flexibility, as well as creative thinking. Therefore, Horváth (2012, 145) concludes that "[…] it is not only the text-specific or culture-specific characteristics of the source message that require creativity from the interpreter, but also the situation-specific features of the act of communication".

While discussing creative behaviour in interpreting Horváth (ibidem) makes yet another interesting observation, namely: the very presence of the interpreters makes the entire communicative situation a little bit unnatural. This is because, even though they themselves constitute elements of this situation, they are neither message senders nor receivers and "they are not fulfilling their own communicational needs". In order to maintain professionalism in these situations, interpreters need to adapt both to the situation and to the participants in such a manner so that they can facilitate communication between them, all of which requires creativity. As stated by Horváth (2012, 145–146):

> "In this sense, creativity implies spontaneous and flexible responses from interpreters taking into account not only the communicational aims of the participants and the setting, but also factors like their personality, motivation, attitudes, emotions, etc. to which they need to adapt. Responding to a situation is based on adapting to the different factors simultaneously. It is true for a given assignment, but we should not forget that there is an infinite variety of interpreting situations and different modes of interpreting which also require adaptability and flexibility in a more general sense on the level of behaviour".

She further rightly observes that interpreting does not only involve the constant need to make linguistic and cultural inferences, but also pragmatic and situational ones. Therefore, contrary to what is true about the written translation, creativity in interpreting should not be limited only to some unusual use of language, since a lot of other aspects involved in interpreting simply cannot be predicted, regardless of how well-prepared and how professional the interpreter is. These factors include (but are not limited to): the participants' personalities, changing agendas, some unforeseen events, etc. It is particularly this level of unpredictability that differentiates between creativity in written translation and creativity in interpreting.

A very interesting example of the interpreter's creativity, flexibility and adaptability to the unpredictable situation is provided by Piotr Krasnowolski – a professional translator and interpreter within the English-Polish language pair, who was already mentioned in subchapter 4.2 of this book – in an interview for Radio Kraków.[55] In this interview he described a situation in which an American speaker took the stage of the Congress Hall in Warsaw, spread his arms and said: "I love it here in Moscow". Krasnowolski admitted that in such a situation the interpreter usually could not know whether the speaker was about to make a joke right after this statement, or whether he was simply tired and had made a mistake. In this case, however, Krasnowolski, who was supposed to interpret this very speaker, had had a chance to spend some time with him that very day, as he had agreed to pick him up from the airport. During the conversation in the car, he found out that the day before the speaker had said exactly the same thing in Moscow, he was very tired and that the same afternoon he would be saying the same words in Bratislava. Thanks to this information, being on stage that day, the interpreter knew for sure that the speaker had made a mistake saying "Moscow" instead of "Warsaw". Therefore, he came up with what could be deemed a very creative solution because, right after the speaker uttered this very sentence, he spread his hands in the same manner as the speaker did, and said in Polish: "Podoba mi się tu bardziej niż w Moskwie" (Eng. "I like it here more than in Moscow"). This may be considered not only a creative solution, but also a very elegant one, as it allowed the speaker to save face. Thanks to his quick and flexible thinking, the interpreter was able to conceal the blunder committed by the speaker and save not only the speaker's face and reputation, but also the entire communicative situation.

Yet another interesting instance of displaying creative behaviour and using flexible thinking when interpreting is offered on the blog rptranslationsword-press.com by Rosado Professional Solutions[56] and it very well illustrates the importance of team work in interpreting. The author of the blog, who is a native Spanish interpreter, reminisces how he was once working in the Spanish booth at a conference in a European country, where the topic of the conference was related to the environment. Delegates from numerous countries attended the very conference and there were interpreters rendering the speeches in many language

---

55 The interview can be watched at: https://www.radiokrakow.pl/wideo/tlumacz-z-krakowa-g wiazda-konkursu-chopinowskiego.

56 https://rpstranslations.wordpress.com/2014/11/21/how-creativity-saved-the-interpretation/, accessed 27.03.2023.

combinations. One day, during the conference, there was a speaker from an English-speaking country, with a very distinctive accent and very specific speaking manner, which the interpreters generally found quite difficult to get used to. During his speech, the blog author (who has just finished his slot of interpreting from English into Spanish and handed the microphone over to his partner), heard a knock on the door of the booth. It turned out to be one of the Italian booth interpreters saying they had a hard time understanding the speaker, and were unable to interpret everything the speaker was saying. Knowing that these interpreters were fairly new, but, at the same time, very dedicated and professional, the Spanish interpreter empathized with them and decided to try his best in order to help them, the more so that the presentation in question was about to last two more hours or so. Therefore, after talking to the Italian interpreter, he found out that her two colleagues in the booth also spoke Spanish and so they decided to apply a relay interpreting rendition as a solution to this problem. In practice this meant that the Spanish booth would take the feed from the floor in English, then interpret it into Spanish, and then the Italian booth would pick up the feed in Spanish and render it into Italian. In the end, this proved to be the best solution. The Spanish interpreter, and the author of the blog, comments that largely thanks to the teamwork, the feeling of camaraderie, as well as willingness to help the fellow interpreters in need, coupled with the experience and skill of both the Spanish and the Italian booths, the solution proved successful and resulted in a seamless delivery of the source language message to both the Spanish- and the Italian-speaking part of the audience. However, as he pointed out, "[t]his would have never happened without the interpreters' professional minds working very fast to find a solution, and without the creativity of the interpreters that made it possible to switch gears in the middle of a very important event already in progress".[57] When commenting on this story, the blog author emphasized the importance of both the interpreter's professionalism and their sense of camaraderie, saying that without them, the two booths in question would have never been able to work together and solve this challenging situation. This story perfectly illustrates how creativity, a fast-working mind, as well as excellent teamwork among colleagues, enabled them to overcome a professional obstacle.

The two stories quoted above illustrate the great significance of creativity, quick thinking and flexible mind in interpreting. Although, as demonstrated in this chapter of the book, an interpreter's creativity might be considered at three main levels – as a product, as a process and as the behaviour – this latter level must not be underestimated since, even though in time certain techniques and strategies may become automated, there will always be some new elements in the

---

57 Ibidem.

situation to which the interpreter would have to adapt and respond flexibly and creatively.

The role of creativity, flexibility and adaptability is neatly summarized by Horváth (2012, 147):

"Interpreting is not seen as out-of-context linguistic encoding-decoding, but rather it is considered as facilitating communication in a more global sense involving paying attention not only to linguistic, but also cultural and situational factors. Selection between alternatives is meant to happen in a linguistic, pragmatic and situational sense. Interpreting can be described as a balancing act in a situation in which the communication that the interpreter is meant to facilitate takes place. To be able to find the right place in such a situation, where the interpreter is not a natural participant in the act of communication, requires a considerable amount of creativity, i.e. adaptability, responsiveness, and flexibility".

One may claim that the awareness and development of creativity might help interpreters to better perform in their job. However, this area of study is still largely unexplored and further research should be done on the creative nature of interpreting.

It cannot be denied that creativity is something that comes in handy not only in the interpreting job (or, in fact, any job), but in numerous situations of everyday life and therefore it is worth developing it and making the most of this amazing creative potential. Ways of doing this will be explored in the following section.

5.2.4 Developing one's Creative Potential

There are certain moments in our life in which we either have to be creative (because someone else requires us to), or simply want to be creative (since we, for instance, have an interesting project to complete, an article to write, a lesson to prepare, or we wish to come up with an original present for our partner). Regardless of whether the motivation is internal or external, there are certain ways in which we all can boost our creative potential, no matter if we are students, teachers or translators/interpreters. Cox (2015, 295–300) suggests the following methods of awakening one's creativity:

Live in the present moment
Creativity is not something that can be maintained at a stable and constant level; rather, it tends to come and go as it pleases. Therefore, it is a good idea to always have a notebook and a pen (or, nowadays, a smartphone will suffice) in order to jot down all creative ideas that may unexpectedly spring to mind. Sometimes,

such moments of sudden inspiration occur at night – we wake up and should immediately note down the idea before we go back to sleep.

Allow yourself to be creative
Sometimes the reasons for our "creativity blocks" are our own inhibitions and limiting thoughts which try to convince us that we are not creative enough or are unable to cope with the task we have been presented with. Therefore, instead of listening to this negative internal monologue, we should immediately start to act. After all, there must have been at least a couple of situations in our life in which we were creative and if we already succeeded a few times, there is no reason why this time should be different.

Find time for relaxation
We are constantly busy and it is virtually impossible to find a moment to distance ourselves from our problems. Our brain is not accustomed to working for long periods of time without a break. Therefore, it is extremely important to have breaks of about 20 minutes after each 90-minute session of work. Our creativity flourishes when we are relaxed.

Immerse yourself or isolate yourself
These are, in fact, two opposite methods of boosting creativity and both of them yield excellent results, depending on the person. The first option is to immerse ourselves completely in what we are doing. If we are planning creative work, we may surround ourselves with anything that stimulates our creative thinking: music, books, paintings, art works or valuable objects which remind us of inspiring people. We can also invite some creative people to join us in our efforts. On the other hand, some people prefer to work alone, in quiet and peaceful environments, where they are completely isolated from other people and all distractions. Whichever option we choose depends on our personality and on the task at hand.

Be tolerant of ambiguity
A lot of people appreciate predictability of things and the related sense of security. Creative thinking, however, does not thrive on predictability but on ambiguity. The best way to learn how to accept ambiguity is analyzing each problem according to the pattern: "On one hand…, on the other hand…".

Find your mental balance
The right frame of mind is crucial to creative thinking. If you feel stressed, worried or upset, you are likely to experience difficulties coming up with new ideas. Therefore, you need to reduce your stress level and achieve the state of

mental balance. One way of doing this is by means of meditation or visualization techniques.[58] Regardless of the method chosen, achieving the state of internal relaxation is fundamental in boosting our creative potential.

Be curious

In order to be creative in various areas of life, we need to be interested in everything. This curiosity can be further divided into three elements:
- attention – look for details, unexpected solutions and everything that you may have missed at the very beginning; the more you notice, the more you develop your creativity;
- asking questions – ask questions even if sometimes the answers seem obvious, as this will often allow you to reach valuable and interesting conclusions;
- sense of wonder – do not take anything for granted, but try to look at things as if you were seeing them for the very first time; this sense of wonder is typical of children who see miracles everywhere, but, unfortunately, it fades as we get older, therefore, it is imperative that we re-learn to see the world as fascinating.

Enlarge the problem, reduce its size, change its shape, turn it upside down

Thinking about what is possible constitutes a part of the creative process. One of the crucial questions in this context is: "What if....?" When you face the challenge of solving a problem, you may use the SCAMPER[59] technique which consists in thinking about what would happen if the given problem was different than it really is. You may ponder over every single aspect of the problem, altering its size and shape and looking at it from various perspectives (e.g. from inside and outside). This technique may be supported by visualization.

Organize a party for creative guests

If you need support in your creative endeavours, you may organize an imaginary party and invite creative and inspirational people. Then imagine what they are saying, how they are behaving, how they are interacting with other guests, which dishes they like the most, what advice they are giving you about your problem. You may find out that following advice of Leonardo da Vinci, Thomas Edison, Walt Disney or Steve Jobs may bring surprising results.

---

58 Examples of such techniques can be found in: Cox, D. 2015. *Kreatywne myślenie dla bystrzaków*. Gliwice: Helion (chapters 6 and 7).
59 The acronym stands for: Substitute, Combine, Adapt, Modify, Put to another use, Eliminate, Reverse.

Sleep creatively

Much of the work done by our brain is done when we are unconscious of it. Our subconscious mind may significantly boost our creative thinking if we only allow it to work. The following are the states in which we gain access to the internal resources of our mind:

- daydreaming – this is a neutral state of mind from which it is relatively easy to enter the alpha state which abounds in various thoughts and images. If you are thinking about a certain problem, it is worth entering this state since it may turn out that the solution is lurking just beneath your conscious mind;
- an energizing nap – a few-minute nap helps us to regain energy and to look at the problem we are facing from a fresh perspective;
- meditation – this is a form of contemplation which supports creative processes;
- sleeping – before falling asleep we may think about the problem we are trying to solve and, should we wake up in the middle of the night, we ought to write down all the dreams and ideas that came to our mind while we were asleep as some of them may provide the solution we have been seeking.

Nowadays, we are all becoming busier and busier, and we rarely decide to make room for creativity in our everyday life. We hardly ever even consider our own creative blueprint, that is a set of factors allowing us to capture creative energy. We all need to realize that boosting our creative skills can be a critical step in reaching our potential, whether in personal or professional life.

Experiencing a moment of creative genius is one of the best feelings we can have, as it provides us with a plethora of positive emotions such as exuberance, joy, satisfaction, pride. Whether we are teachers looking for an inspiration, translators/interpreters wishing to develop a flexible mind or students trying desperately to find motivation to study, we can all access our creative potential and ignite our creative fire. Regardless of the method we select, enhancing our creativity is bound to improve all aspects of our personal and professional lives.

Chapter 6:
Interpreters: Training and Profession

6.1   Translator and Interpreter Training in Poland

In the past, translators were perceived as creators of literature and were enjoying equal rights with the very authors. Later, however, the status of translators changed radically together with the gradual professionalization of their occupation. Nowadays, a translator is no longer recognized as a mediator offering a guide to the original literary work, but rather as a professional involved in a quite specific form of communication (Tabakowska 1998/2001, 531).

Translation was first institutionalized in Poland in 1976 – it was then that the Translators' Commission of the Union of Polish Writers was established. Five years later another organization was founded – the Association of Polish Translators and Interpreters. In 1990 the Polish Society of Sworn and Specialized Translators (TEPIS) was set up, which, together with the two previously mentioned bodies, is a member of the International Federation of Translators. If was founded in order to train specialist translators in response to the demands of the political and economic changes in Poland. TEPIS's aims are:

- "To represent the interests of legal translators and court interpreters and enhance their status by its actions as a public benefit organization, entitled to cooperate with the government to perform public tasks;
- To develop, compile, edit and publish specialized materials with the purpose of enriching legal translators' and court interpreters' professional knowledge and to propagate among them other information of interest;
- To offer opportunities for the continuing professional development of legal translators' and court interpreters' qualifications by holding training courses, meetings, seminars, etc."[60]

---

60 https://tepis.org.pl/the-polish-society-of-sworn-and-specialized-translators/, accessed 31.03. 2023.

However, as claimed by Tabakowska (1998/2001, 531), although the demand for professional translation services is on the increase in Poland, translator training is still inadequate in this country. One of the possible reasons is that translation is not a regulated profession (apart from the profession of a sworn translator), which means that there are no legal regulations which would stipulate formal requirements for the candidates for this profession, including the level of education (Klimkowska 2013, 45). Hence the education market in Poland offers numerous and various forms of translation and interpretation training, from BA studies, to postgraduate and specialized courses.

There are four main forms of translator and interpreter training available in Poland (ibidem):
– undergraduate studies;
– graduate studies;
– specialized postgraduate studies;
– specialized courses.

As regards undergraduate translation studies, they are conducted full-time and part-time by universities, academies and other institutes of higher education within the faculty of philology. However, this form of training does not seem to be sufficient as translation and interpreting require a separate study profile. In the 1990s Tabakowska (1992, 15) postulated developing comprehensive translation programmes at the institutes of higher education. There has been some progress made in this area since then but, as observed by Zieliński (2005, 429), there is still room for improvement. He states that when analyzing curricula at faculties of neophilology, one cannot help noticing that teaching translation constitutes a more or less accidental addition, sometimes in the form of practical classes, sometimes practical classes combined with general lectures and sometimes is non-existent altogether. He emphasizes the fact that a very small number of hours is devoted to translation, which is one of the reasons why translation competences acquired during neophilological studies still leave a lot to be desired (Zieliński 2005, 429).

Also Hejwowski noticed problems in the area of translator training in Poland. He states that some translation teachers are not fully aware of the complexity of their task and they wrongly assume that it is sufficient to enrich a typical philology course with some specialist languages in order to train translators of specialist texts (2004, 167). There is still a misconception in Poland, according to which being a philologist is tantamount to being a translator (Klimkowska 2013, 46).

Therefore, on the basis of the range of translational education, one can differentiate between the following types of higher education courses (ibidem):

- neophilological studies without the translation profile but having in their curricula a few translation subjects;
- neophilological studies offering translation specialization or translation major (a general one);
- studies in translation offering narrow professional specializations, for instance audiovisual translation, literary translation, simultaneous interpreting, specialist translation, etc.

As observed by Klimkowska (ibidem), only the second and the third of the enumerated types (and the latter in particular) allow the students to develop specialist competences in translation and/or interpreting. The notion of translator competence is defined by Kiraly as a complex set of creative, largely intuitive, socially embedded and multifaceted skills and abilities (2000, 49). Therefore, according to him, the major objectives of translator/interpreter education should be:
- increasing the students' awareness of phenomena related to translation/interpreting;
- assisting the students in developing translator/interpreter self-awareness;
- helping the students to create customized tools that would allow each student to function well after graduating, as a translator/interpreter.

Kiraly considers translator/interpreter education to be much more than purely linguistic training. According to him, translator/interpreter competence includes psychosocial subcompetence as well, which means that the translator/interpreter has the following: self-awareness, self-control, willingness to introspect and to reflect on his/her decisions, the ability to function well within the society (ibidem). This means that the translator/interpreter training should be of an interdisciplinary character. Even a high level of linguistic and translation competences will not guarantee that the translator/interpreter will be providing top quality service and achieve professional success if he/she is not prepared in the psychopedagogical dimension as well. A good translator/interpreter needs to have time- and stress-management skills, know his/her strengths and limitations, be prepared to establish professional relations with the translation commissioners, clients and other business partners (Klimkowska 2013, 47). All these psychosocial competences, together with excellent communication skills, are nowadays a must if one is to achieve success in this profession.

However, also as significant as psychosocial competences is having "the right" degree. Solarczyk-Ambrozik (2004, 171) emphasizes the fact that the most important factors determining one's competitive advantage on the job market are: the graduate's competences and their professional preparation, as well as having a degree of a particular university. As illustrated by the results of her research, the features that are desired by the prospective employers include: higher education, experience, good command of foreign languages, creativity, ability to work well in a team, communication skills (ibidem). All this applies to translation/interpreting graduates as well, and although the requirement of knowing foreign languages is fulfilled by their very profile of studies, by itself it is definitely not enough to ensure professional success.

As regards interpreter training in particular, Tryuk (2007, 148) observes that it was first largely based on the experience and intuition of practising interpreters who, until the 1990s, were using intuitive teaching methods which only rarely were verified in terms of their effectiveness. What is also interesting is that, at that time, professional interpreters were often unwilling to take up the teaching job, sometimes due to their lack of teaching competences, and sometimes simply for fear of having to train the next generations of the potential competitors on the job market.

According to Keiser (1987, after Tryuk 2007, 148–149), the interpreter training should provide the future interpreter with the feeling of confidence that, on completion of the course, the interpreter will be able to successfully complete his/her first interpreting assignment. In order for this to happen, an interpreter training course, as postulated by Keiser, should imitate as closely as possible real-life conditions and should be conducted by practising conference interpreters. Therefore, instructors and educators need to use authentic materials and arrange didactic situations that would closely resemble ones experienced by professional interpreters on a daily basis.

The initial stage of an interpreter training is recruitment during which candidates are tested in order to verify their interpreting skills, as well as the general aptitude for the profession. Such a competence test checks if the candidate has the following (Longley 1989, after Tryuk 2007, 149):

– a very good command of the languages the candidate is going to be working with;
– an ability to quickly understand and transfer the source text message, regardless of which of the two languages it was formulated in;
– an ability to memorize logical links between parts of the text;
– an ability to deliver the message in a pleasant and confident voice;
– a broad general knowledge, inquisitiveness and the willingness to learn new things;
– an ability to work well in a team;
– an ability to work in stressful conditions.

A well-designed competence test typically includes certain tasks and exercises that test all these above-mentioned abilities and personality traits.

As regards the actual interpreter training, most training courses encompass the following components (Gile 2001, after Tryuk 2007, 150–151):

- the knowledge component, including language training, with a particular emphasis on specialist languages, as well as thematic training encompassing subject areas within which the candidate will be interpreting;
- the know-how component (related to conference interpreting) that can be further divided into:
  a) methodological-strategic subcomponent (knowing the norms, ways of solving particular interpreting-related problems, techniques of preparation for the conference, note-taking techniques);
  b) cognitive subcomponent (effort management, dividing the effort between the stages of listening, analysis, memorization and production);
  c) linguistic subcomponent (an ability to avoid interference, to construct logical and correct sentences while having divided attention and an ability to use problem-solving strategies).

Tryuk (2007, 151) observes that the interpreting curricula differ from each other in terms of duration, their contents, division between individual components and their role, methods of teaching, types of activities and exercises, forms of assessment, etc. However, she is adamant that in the interpreter training the instructors should focus on the evaluation rather than testing, as well as on the process rather than the final product. In order to be able to do that, one needs to first specify the evaluation criteria, as well as competences of an interpreter, and here there are various approaches, depending on the scholar formulating them. For instance, Van Hoof (1962, after Tryuk 2007, 151) mentions physical attributes such as resistance to stress; intellectual ones like excellent command of the languages in question, as well as a broad general knowledge; and mental ones, for example memory, concentration, split attention. Another view on the interpreter's competence is represented by Kopczyński (1981, after Tryuk 2007, 152), who states that it encompasses excellent written and oral command of the languages between which one is interpreting, ease in formulating one's thoughts, empathy towards the speaker, good memory and reliable note-taking techniques (for consecutive interpreting), split attention, resistance to stress, an ability to quickly react to the changing circumstances, as well as an ability to rapidly introduce the necessary corrections and modifications to the target text.

Interestingly enough, certain scholars, such as Hoffman (1997), understand the development of competences as the development of expertise that can be divided into the following levels:

- the level of a layman, i.e. a person who knows nothing about a given field;
- the level of a novice, i.e. someone who has completed some preliminary training in a given field;

- the level of an apprentice, i.e. a person who is undergoing further stages of training;
- the level of a journeyman, i.e. someone who is allowed to perform their professional duties without supervision;
- the level of an expert, i.e. a person capable of successfully dealing with some unusual tasks;
- the level of a master, i.e. someone who is prepared and ready to teach others.

When commenting on these levels, Tryuk (2007:154) refers to the opinion stated by Gile (2001) who said that the aim of process-oriented assessment is not so much the optimization of the product's quality (i.e. the translated text), but rather the very course of the process itself. Hence, this kind of evaluation also needs to be supported by product-oriented assessment, with the final assessment checking if the student has fulfilled all the training aims assumed.

According to Tryuk (ibidem), interpreter training should be based on rules and parameters used in the assessment of a professional interpreter. What these rules and parameters entail will be discussed in the following subchapter.

6.2 Norms in Interpreting

As pointed out by Kruk-Junger (2016, 42), there are certain major aspects related to the interpreting job which illustrate the kind of difficulties that the interpreters need to face, and these might be divided into the following groups:
- the context (time and place of the assignment, the level of comfort and stress etc.);
- the sender and the receiver (their attitude, knowledge, expectations);
- the original code (terminology, register, form) and message (logic, speech rate, length etc.);
- the interpreter (their knowledge, competences, experience, motivation etc.);
- the second code (terminology, correctness, translation techniques) and message (the strategy selected, form of translation and content);
- the channel (noise level, technical conditions, quality of contact).

Kruk-Junger (2016, 43) further observes that the quality in interpreting should not be measured by the same standards that have been established for other forms of translation, as here the success is going to be largely determined by the interpreter's adaptation of the message to all of the factors affecting a certain interpreting situation.

Quality assessment in interpreting is based on a certain consensus of what is "good" and "bad" in interpreting practice and this consensus, in turn, is based on specific linguistic (semantic) and extralinguistic (pragmatic) criteria. According to Tryuk (2007, 157), such a consensus is called a norm in interpreting. However, various scholars offer slightly different ideas of what these norms should be.

For instance, Viaggio (1999) proposes the following norms:
- norms related to the interpretation process, concerning interpretation techniques and strategies;
- norms related to the interpretation product, concerning the form of the end product;
- norms related to the users' expectations, i.e. the interpretation listeners;
- professional norms concerning interpreters' professional conduct.

However, taking into consideration the division between conference and community interpreting, Tryuk (2007, 159) suggested the following norms:
- norms related to the expectations of the interpretation users, including the faithfulness, comprehensibility, fluency and linguistic accuracy;
- interpreters' professional norms, i.e. behaviour that is adequate to the situation, interpreter's neutrality, impartiality and objectivity, resistance to stress;
- situational norms which are particularly important, for instance, in community interpreting when the interpreter, apart from transferring the information from the source to the target language, also plays a role of a dialogue coordinator.

Similar aspects are mentioned by the AIIC,[61] whose norms specified for conference interpreters include:
- comprehensibility of the target text;
- successful conveyance of the source language speaker's intention;
- speech fluency;
- successful conveyance of the speaker's tone and beliefs.

In line with the above-mentioned norms, Tryuk (2007, 161) claims that interpreting is not about transferring the message word-for-word, but rather about conveying the message together with its entire semantic, connotative and aesthetic dimension via linguistic means (lexical, syntactic and stylistic ones) of the target language. Interpreting is mostly about understanding the speaker's intention, and hence it is important to be able to detach from the original wording and convey the subtle intention of the speaker via the target language words and

---

61 AIIC – Intentional Association of Conference Interpreters, https://aiic.org/site/home?nav=home.

structures. Therefore, taking the above into consideration, and according to the AIIC, the following norms are the most important (after Tryuk 2007, 161):
– the norm of conveying the speaker's intention in the most comprehensible way possible;
– the norm of creating a certain form of communication.

A list of norms for interpretation product and service, which an interpreter should be directed by, includes the following aspects (Viezzi 1996, 40):
– fidelity (towards the source message);
– adequacy (of the target language expression);
– equivalence (of the intended effect);
– success (of the communicative interaction).

Yet another division of norms in interpreting is offered by Harris (1990):[62]
1. The interpreter should speak in the 1st person singular as if he/she was the speaker. This means that if the speaker says "I'm happy to be here," the interpreter will also say "I'm happy to be here", only in the target language, instead of "Mr. X says he's happy to be here". Harris (ibidem) postulates that this is one of the first aspects that the interpretation students need to be made aware of and told to be consistent about.
2. As regards professional simultaneous interpreting, the norm is that that if the original speech lasts more than 20 minutes, it is typically rendered by a succession of several interpreters who take it in turns to interpret its successive fragments. Harris (ibidem) comments on this by saying that the audience listening to the original hear only one voice and the idiolect of only one person, while those who listen to the interpretation hear several different voices with different manners of delivery, which may disturb their experience. This disturbing effect may also be produced when, for instance, the speaker is a man and the first interpreter is also a man, but then a woman takes over the interpreting. Also, as pointed out by Harris, it rarely happens that the speaker's and the interpreter's voices and personalities match, so, for instance, an elderly male speaker may be interpreted into a young, female voice. To provide a counter example to such situations, and an example for others to follow, Harris mentions the French literary TV program Apostrophesý, where for guests who do not speak French, simultaneous interpretation is provided. However, they carefully choose the interpreter, making sure that his or her voice matches the appearance and character of the guest. Therefore, they achieve a very realistic result that resembles watching a dubbed film. Hence,

---

62 https://www.researchgate.net/publication/263550981_Norms_in_Interpretation, accessed 4.04.2023.

Harris observes that perhaps TV interpreting is going to develop different norms from the established ones of conference interpreting.

3. The norm in Western European interpreter schools is that conference interpreters should only work into their A language (i. e. their native language). However, according to Harris (ibidem), this is unrealistic and impractical since interpreting situations frequently require interpreters to work into the second language (B) as well, and hence the students should be taught to interpreter in both these directions. One possible reason why it is postulated that the interpreter work into their mother tongue is that if they do this into their second language, it may not be so pleasant for the audience to listen to it. Nevertheless, Harris observes this norm does not really work in most court interpreting situations, as there is typically only one interpreter to serve everybody. Also, it would not be practical in places where there is a shortage of native-speaker interpreters into foreign languages.

4. Norms related to the acceptability of the target language production. Because interpreting is typically performed at a significant speed and cannot be revised before delivery, mistakes will inevitably occur. Harris (ibidem) mentions his colleague's idea to speed up the interpretation by replacing the regular translators with a team of secretaries who would transcribe tape recordings of the simultaneous interpreters. This idea was put into practice but it soon became obvious that it was very troublesome to edit the transcribed interpretations to publishable standards than to translate directly from edited transcripts of the original speeches.

Apart from enumerating the above-mentioned norms in interpreting, Harris (ibidem) also mentions the oppositions sated by Savory in *The Art of Translation:*

1. The interpreter shall speak in the first person, or the interpreter shall speak in the third person.
2. The interpreter follows the level of excitement, tone of voice, even the gestures, of the speaker, or the interpreter remains calm and neutral.
3. The interpreter may neither add to nor omit from the original, or the interpreter may add and omit, according to the circumstances.

Apart from all the above-mentioned norms, Harris (ibidem) mentions one more which, according to him, is even more fundamental and universal, and it says that people who speak on behalf of others, including the interpreters, need to re-express the original speakers' ideas and the manner of expressing them as accurately as possible and without major omissions, and they should not include their own ideas and expressions. This norm, however, is so obvious, it does not need to be explicitly stated anywhere. It is only when an exception appears that the professional interpreters are made aware of the very rule, and this may happen, as observed by Harris (ibidem), for instance when an interpreting student asks what they should do if the speaker has made a mistake or is expressing some offensive or embarrassing views or ideas.

As regards the sources of norms applying to interpreters, there are certain legal documents regulating the profession and interpreters' responsibilities, such as the law regarding sworn translation, copyrights, and regulations regarding confidentiality (Kruk-Junger 2016, 44). These documents focus mostly on the non-linguistic aspects of interpreting.

In Poland, sworn translation is regulated by the act of 2004 (Dz. U. z 2015 r., poz. 487)[63] and by the code of practice proposed by TEPiS,[64] both of which may serve as sources of guidelines for practising translators and interpreters, particularly in terms of professional conduct and obligations towards clients.

The copyright in Poland is regulated by the act of 1994 (Dz. U. z 2006 r. nr 90, poz. 631).[65] Even though the final product of the interpretation is not recorded in any way, it is also protected by the copyright law, with the same legal effects as contracts and payments (ibidem).

As regards confidentiality issues, these concern the area of personal data (the personal data protection act of 1997 (Dz. U. z 2014 r. poz. 1182)[66] and classified information (the 2010 law on protection of classified information (Dz. U. z 2010 r. nr 182, poz. 1228).[67] These regulations may serve as guidelines for interpreters to establishing relations with their clients.

However, as observed by Kruk-Junger (2016, 46), the norms specified in the above-mentioned documents are insufficient to solve all of the interpreter's problems. Hence, adapting norms related to other fields of study may prove useful here. For instance, the theories concerning cultural differences, proposed by Edward Hall (1976) and Geert Hofstede (2001) may help interpreters to tackle certain problems that stem from cultural differences and concern, for instance, expectations and attitudes of the client or non-verbal communication. Understanding and acknowledging cultural differences may help interpreters become successful mediators, should the need arise.

Certain norms and good practices may also be adapted from the field of business communication, for example ones related to the area of ethics and etiquette. They could be applied to the interpreter-client relationship (Kruk-Junger 2016, 46).

Seeing the need to introduce a special course on professional ethics and etiquette for translation and interpretation students, Kruk-Junger designed one

---

63 https://isap.sejm.gov.pl/isap.nsf/DocDetails.xsp?id=WDU20150000487.
64 https://tepis.org.pl/kodeks-tlumacza-przysieglego/.
65 https://isap.sejm.gov.pl/isap.nsf/DocDetails.xsp?id=wdu20060900631.
66 https://isap.sejm.gov.pl/isap.nsf/DocDetails.xsp?id=wdu20140001182.
67 https://isap.sejm.gov.pl/isap.nsf/DocDetails.xsp?id=WDU20101821228.

and implemented it at the Tischner European University in Cracow in 2013. The curriculum that she proposed included the following modules (Kruk-Junger 2016, 48–49):

a.   Introduction (including the concepts of ethics, etiquette, morality, professionalism, interpreting as a type of communication, forms of interpreting);
b.   Interpreting as an interaction (work conditions, problems and interferences in communication);
c.   The interpreter's role in communication (theoretical approaches including the Skopos theory, existing codes of ethics);
d.   The law in interpreters' work, part one (the legal status of interpreters in selected countries);
e.   The law in interpreters' work, part two (regulations related to interpreters' work in Poland, including sworn translations, copyright issues, privacy laws, confidentiality);
f.   Etiquette, part one (behaviour in everyday communication, the culture of language and non-verbal communication);
g.   Etiquette, part two (differences in social and business etiquette, appropriate behaviour at work and business dress codes, professional standards);
h.   Relations between client(s) and the interpreter (expectations of clients, interpreter's reaction to issues like criticism, aggression and manipulation);
i.   Solving ethical problems (activities where students come up with their own solutions to certain problems);
j.   Mistakes (interpreting techniques and strategies, interpreting errors and *faux pas*);
k.   Cultural differences (different cultures and ethical postures, the role of the interpreter as a cultural mediator, culture-generated communication problems, culture-related differences in etiquette and ethics);
l.   Revision and conclusions (professional conduct as a result of the assumed etiquette, ethics and moral convictions of the interpreter);
m.   Final exam.

The above description demonstrates that the course includes a wide variety of the existing norms for interpreting, from the formal legal obligations and codes of ethics, to the cultural norms which derive from some general rules of professional conduct. Kruk-Junger designed it as an addition to language-focused ones and therefore her course concentrates more on the extra-linguistic aspects of interpreters' work. When talking about interpreter training, Kruk-Junger (2016, 50) says:

"It could be argued that the interpreter training should stop promoting norms that come strictly form the 'just translate' approach and concentrate more on other, more practical and realistic guidelines, as, for example, the ones proposed by Niska or the Skopos theory. It should therefore include elements that will prepare the students to solve the most common problems according to high ethical standards and tackle such aspects as the role of the interpreter in communication, work conditions, the legal boundaries of the work of interpreters, ethical guidelines, business etiquette, assertiveness, cultural differences, the expectations of clients, taking responsibility for the consequences of one's actions etc. Only then can we expect interpreters to be true professionals, able to deal with everyday problems in an ethical and dignified manner, and last but not least, to take full responsibility for the communication process, both in ensuring its success or, otherwise, taking the responsibility for its failure".

Taking into consideration all the norms discussed in this subchapter, as well as the suggested course designed for aspiring interpreters, it seems worth mentioning the opinion stated by Cartellieri (1983, 213) who said that interpretation quality assessment is heavily dependent of the assessing person; it would differ significantly according to whether the evaluating person is an experienced colleague or an interpretation commissioner. The assessment is also going to depend strongly on the context in which the interpreting assignment takes place. Therefore, according to him, there can be no universally accepted definition of interpretation quality, only an approximate one, as quality is a variable dependent on the given culture, social group and language community.

6.3 Professional Associations of Interpreters

Conference interpreters started establishing some professional associations only after the Second World War and the following factors contributed to this (Tryuk 2007, 171):

- the establishment of numerous regional and national organizations, which might have resulted in the interpreter profession being closed within the borders of one country, region, continent, which entail limited mobility; since this profession is international by nature, its practice should know no borders, and hence there was a need for interpreters to be organised as a single international body rather than as a federation of national groups;
- imposition of unfavourable work conditions by large organizations hiring conference interpreters;
- the necessity to introduce professional rules and remuneration systems for interpreters employed full-time in various institutions, as well as those who worked freelance.

The only global association of conference interpreters is the International Association of Conference Interpreters – AIIC[68] (AIIC – Association Internationale des Interprètes de Conférence), founded in 1953 when interpreting profession was still in its infancy. It represents over 3,000 members present in over 100 countries and its secretariat is in Geneva. Candidates applying for membership need to abide by the rules stipulated in AIIC's Code of Ethics and Professional Standards.[69] Although members of the AIIC are organized in regions by place of residence, membership is portable and even when an interpreter changes the country of residence, membership is preserved.

Since its establishment, AIIC has been continually promoting high standards of quality and ethics in the profession and representing the interests of interpreting professionals. The organization has been involved in all areas related to conference interpreting and is working for the benefit of all conference interpreters and for the entire profession. AIIC sets high professional and ethical standards and promotes the working conditions that high quality interpreting requires. The organization also contributes its expertise as far as interpreter training is concerned, ensuring that it conforms to the highest standards. AIIC has a strict admissions procedure, which is based on a peer review system, and the candidates applying for membership must be sponsored by interpreters who have been AIIC members for at least five years. AIIC members are required to abide by the association's code of ethics and its professional standards.

There are three main sectors within the AIIC:[70]
- the Agreement Sector, gathering interpreters working for the major international organizations with which AIIC has negotiated collective agreements;
- the Private Market Sector, being a forum for freelancers and consultant interpreters working for non-institutional clients;
- Staff Interpreters' Committee, bringing together members who are employed full-time in national or international bodies.

AIIC projects aim to advance the profession and to build on past achievements through research, cooperation among trainers, outreach and communication. The main tasks of AIIC are:[71]
- negotiating collective agreements with major international organizations, governing terms and conditions of employment;
- keeping up-to-date with market developments through the work of the Private Market Sector;

---

68 Official website: https://aiic.org/.
69 The document is available at: https://aiic.org/document/10277/CODE_2022_E&F_final.pdf.
70 https://web.archive.org/web/20200711024824/https://aiic.net/page/1673/aiic-an-inclusive-and -representative-professional-body/lang/1, accessed 7.04.2023.
71 https://web.archive.org/web/20200711024855/https://aiic.net/page/1280, accessed 7.04.2023.

- representing all conference interpreters and engaging in a long-term project, in collaboration with UNESCO, on the definition and recognition of the interpreting profession;
- establishing standards in cooperation with normative bodies, such as the International Organization for Standardization (ISO). AIIC also provides expert guidance to architects designing conference centres;
- promoting professional excellence and protecting working conditions, as AIIC has at its disposal a large corpus of information about the optimum conditions for quality interpretation;
- advocating best practice in training through its survey of interpreting schools and sponsorship of continuing education courses;
- communicating with users; in 1990s the AIIC commissioned a detailed study of user expectations,[72] which demonstrated the importance of certain quality criteria, such as sense consistency with the original and logical cohesion. Also significant proved to be form-related quality parameters of correct terminology, correct grammar and appropriate style. Delivery-related criteria, in contrast, were attributed a lower degree of importance – except for the criterion of fluency. However, it needs to be mentioned that in this particular aspect the degree of importance attributed to various quality criteria varies in relation to the meeting (type of event, degree of formality, duration and size) and the domain (political, diplomatic, business, legal, medical) in which the event takes place;
- maintaining communication with the community of interpreters;
- reaching out to newcomers through regional seminars, providing useful information, and the Young AIIC Interpreters Group (YAIN);
- promoting the use of languages in a multilingual world through its projects and direct action in international bodies;
- keeping abreast of new technologies and responding to the challenges and opportunities they entail.

In Poland, the largest association of translators and interpreters is The Polish Society of Sworn and Specialized Translators TEPIS.[73] It is a public benefit organization, founded in 1990 by a group of members of the Association of Polish Translators and Interpreters, and today it is a member of the International Federation of Translators (FIT) and of the European Legal Interpreters and Translators Association (EULITA). The main aim of the organization is to represent interests of legal translators and court interpreters, as well as provide opportunities for their professional development, for instance by organizing

---

72 https://aiic.org/document/9646/, accessed 7.04.2023.
73 https://tepis.org.pl/.

training courses and workshops. Also, TEPIS publishes specialized materials aimed at broadening the knowledge of translators and interpreters. According to the information stated on its official website, in 2019 the TEPIS Society had around 800 members. TEPIS offices can be found in Szczecin, Wrocław, Kraków, Bytom, Białystok and Poznań.

The tasks that the organization is going to undertake in the future include:[74]

- "to persuade the Polish legislator that – according to item 11 of the 1976 UNESCO Recommendation on the legal protection of translators and translations – it is necessary to provide for them a statutory duty to be taught translation skills and techniques irrespective of the requirement to pass a state examination in order to be appointed a sworn translator;
- to make the Minister of Justice aware of the fact that average official rates for court interpreting and legal translators' services are much below the European standards and need to be increased;
- to make the Minister of Justice aware of the EC recommendation that there is a distinct difference between the profession of an interpreter and a translator that should be provided by Polish law;
- to improve international judicial cooperation and the exchange of best practices with the support of the European Legal Interpreters and Translators Association (EU-LITA)".

---

74 https://tepis.org.pl/the-polish-society-of-sworn-and-specialized-translators/, accessed 8.04. 2023.

Chapter 7:
Practical Exercises and Activities

This chapter is going to provide some ideas for practical activities and exercises to be introduced in the classroom with interpretation students. They have been compiled on the basis of: Chmiel, Agnieszka and Przemysław Janikowski (eds.). 2015. *Dydaktyka tłumaczenia ustnego*. Katowice: Stowarzyszenie Inicjatyw Wydawniczych.

7.1 Consecutive Interpreting

7.1.1 Memory and Visualization Exercises[75]

Exercise 1: Shopping

Aim: practising visualization
The teacher asks the students to create a shopping list. Students suggest ten products which are then written down on the board. The group then collectively proceeds to visualize a story in which the items on the shopping list appear in unusual contexts.

The teacher selects individual suggestions (the weirder, the better) and asks the group to imagine a story. For example, if the first products on the list are milk, cereal and paper towels, the students are instructed not to create a conventional story (for instance, with the protagonist getting up in the morning, having milk with cereal for breakfast and using a paper towel to wipe up the spilled milk), but rather use their imagination and come up with, for example, the following story: A milk carton wakes up in bed in the morning, stretches its tiny arms, gets up and

---

75 On the basis of: Chmiel, Agnieszka. "Rozdział 6: Pamięć w tłumaczeniu konsekutywnym". In: Chmiel, Agnieszka and Przemysław Janikowski (eds.). 2015. *Dydaktyka tłumaczenia ustnego*. Katowice: Stowarzyszenie Inicjatyw Wydawniczych, pp. 125–140. Sample texts provided for these exercises are in Polish but the teacher may also select some English texts.

goes to the bathroom to take a shower which, instead of water, pours cereals. The milk carton makes a turban on its head with a paper towel and comes out of the bathroom, shaking off the last cereals.

The teacher should encourage students to imagine many details (e. g. milk of a specific brand) and to use multiple senses (not only sight, but also hearing and smell). After the story has been created, the teacher covers the list of products on the board and asks the students to recreate it on pieces of paper. The aim is to remember all or almost all of the products in the correct order. The teacher may check during the next week's class if the students still remember the items. Thus, they learn the power of visualization as an effective mnemonic technique.

Exercise 2: Pyramid of cans

Aims: practising visualization, analyzing the structure of the text
The teacher presents the group with about one-minute easy-to-visualize texts divided into categories: topography (for example, a travelogue that allows the students to imagine a map or the places described), a process (for example: a recipe, instructions for assembling a simple device, a manufacturing process) or a series of events (for example, an accident report).

Students imagine as many content elements of a given text as possible and reconstruct or translate it without notes. The texts should be quite easy at the beginning and should not include too many details.

A sample text:
Godzina ósma rano. Szklane drzwi Centrum Handlowego Reduta za chwilę się otworzą. Do środka jak zwykle wchodzi grupa łowców okazji. Omijają wszystkie sklepy, przemierzając puste i senne alejki, zmierzają do supermarketu, który dziś oferuje ciekawe promocje. Starsza pani w berecie i z kraciastą torbą na kółkach szuka kompletu garnków za 19,99 zł, który wcześniej widziała w gazetce reklamowej. W końcu znajduje i pakuje do wózka cały zestaw aluminiowych garnków z czarnymi uchwytami. Obok garnków piętrzy się piramida kukurydzy konserwowej i groszku w promocyjnej cenie. Emerytka wkłada do wózka kilka puszek. Przy kasie stoi w kolejce za otyłym mężczyzną w roboczym stroju, który kupuje bułki i serek topiony. Po zapłaceniu za zakupy emerytka wychodzi z centrum i udaje się na pobliski przystanek autobusowy. Wydaje się zadowolona ze złowionych okazji.

Exercise 3: Optical cleaning

Aims: practising visualization and public speaking
The teacher shows the students a sample structure of a simple speech:

Introduction:
- may contain a surprising statement to attract the listeners' attention;
- features the topic and purpose of the speech;
- may include justification as to why this particular speaker discusses this topic.

Main body:
- contains individual elements of the speech as separate points.

Conclusion:
- summary;
- may contain the speaker's direct address to the listeners.

The teacher then presents the group with a simple text corresponding to this structure. The task of the group is to remember and reconstruct/translate the text by memorizing key words (a maximum of about three key words for the introduction, one for each main body point, about one or two key words for the conclusion).

In the next part of the exercise, the teacher suggests topics for the students' presentations. Students prepare them in accordance with the previously discussed structure and present them for reconstruction/translation based on keywords.

A sample text:
Czy zdarzyło się Wam w panice sprzątać swój pokój w akademiku po sobotniej imprezie, bo zauważyliście z okna, że właśnie z samochodu wysiadają wasi rodzice, aby złożyć wam niespodziewaną niedzielną wizytę? Jeśli tak, to z pewnością zainteresuje was temat sprzątania optycznego, o którym chcę wam dzisiaj opowiedzieć. Sprzątanie optyczne to takie sprzątanie, którego celem jest stworzenie wrażenia porządku w bardzo krótkim czasie. Mam w tym doświadczenie, ponieważ przez całe studia mieszkałem w akademiku. Przedstawię wam trzy metody sprzątania optycznego. Po pierwsze, puste butelki pozostałe po sobotniej imprezie można wrzucić pod łóżko. Warunkiem efektywności tej metody jest posiadanie długiej kołdry lub koca, które zakryją spód łóżka. Po drugie, brudne ubrania można sprytnie wrzucić pod czyste i w ten sposób stworzyć wrażenie porządku i czystości. Po trzecie, brudne naczynia włożyć można do szafki pod zlewem, licząc na to, że rodzice akurat nie będą wyrzucać nic do śmietniczki. Przedstawione powyżej trzy metody optycznego sprzątania pustych butelek, brudnych ubrań i naczyń można bardzo łatwo zastosować. Mam nadzieję, że przydadzą się wam przy najbliższej nieoczekiwanej wizycie waszych rodziców lub potencjalnej sympatii, na której chcecie zrobić dobre wrażenie.

Sample key words:
rodzice, sprzątanie optyczne, akademik (introduction),
butelki, ubrania, naczynia (main body),
wrażenie (conclusion).

Exercise 4: Last minute

Aims: memory training, building lexical resources
The teacher informs the students that they will receive a glossary at short notice, which they should get familiar with in order to be able translate a text later on in class. The teacher sends the glossary a day or two before the class, but it can also be a few hours before the class if the students are able to receive it in an electronic form. At the beginning of the class, the teacher tests the students' knowledge of this vocabulary and then the students proceed to a traditional consecutive interpretation of the text featuring this vocabulary.

Activity 5: Sponge

Aims: memory training, broadening specialist knowledge
The teacher informs the students that the texts to be interpreted during the next class will focus on a specific specialist topic (e.g. the operation of a biological sewage treatment plant or the controversy around vaccinations). Students not only prepare vocabulary, but also research the given topic. In class, students can be asked to present what they have learned before interpreting the prepared text (these mini-presentations can also serve as texts for interpreting).

Exercise 6: The news

Aim: memory training
The teacher encourages students to watch at least one major news programme every day. After watching a 20–25-minute programme, students try to recall its content – first the topics of the audiovisual material, then as much detail as possible about each news item. This exercise also engages visual memory. The students should be able to notice that when reconstructing the news, they recalled the images they had previously seen on the screen. For verification, students can be advised to record the programmes they watch (or to use the recordings of the programmes posted on the Internet) and compare the recalled information with the content of the programmes.

7.1.2   Note-taking Exercises[76]

Exercise 1: Moving weights

Aim: developing the ability to analyze the structure of the text, memory training, optimizing the layout of notes
Students are asked to listen to the speech in a foreign language divided into about one-minute chunks. While listening, they are not allowed to take notes, they are supposed to focus on the text as if they were about to interpret it from memory. However, after each passage they receive extra time in which they have to take notes and, when they are ready, to start interpreting on the basis of them. After the translation of the entire text, there is a discussion in which students assess the difficulty level and specify those elements which are easier to memorize and those which are better noted down. They may also discuss the layout and structure of their notes.

Exercise 2: In search of structure

Aims: developing the ability to analyze the structure of the text and text condensation
Students are asked to bring larger sheets of paper to class (at least A4 format). They receive a transcript of a few-minute speech which includes digressions, unfinished sentences, comparisons based on parallelisms, etc. On the basis of the first few sentences the teacher explains the rules of verticalism in note-taking, and asks students to do the same for the remaining sentences. After the task is completed, the text is discussed element by element, with particular focus on structure markers (conjunctions, pauses, repetitions, deictic expressions, intonation etc., but also non-verbal elements, if available) that would allow for the recognition of macro- and microstructure.

Exercise 3: Labelling

Aims: developing split attention, memory training, developing condensation skills, practising the use of symbols, analyzing the structure of the text
Students listen to 2–3 minute fragments of a text in their native language, without taking notes. After listening, students have the opportunity to note down a limited number of words and symbols, for example ten, seven or five (the dif-

---

76 On the basis of: Janikowski, Przemysław. "Rozdział 7: Notowanie". In: Chmiel, Agnieszka and Przemysław Janikowski (eds.). 2015. *Dydaktyka tłumaczenia ustnego*. Katowice: Stowarzyszenie Inicjatyw Wydawniczych, pp. 142–166.

ficulty level can be adjusted). After the note-taking phase, each student reproduces the text in the same language.

Exercise 4: Impure language

Aims: developing the ability to analyze the structure of the text
Students receive one longer text in their native language, divided into fragments of no more than two minutes, and are asked to interpret it according to the following rules: the first three fragments – no specific rules; the next five fragments – note-taking only in the source language; the next three fragments – no specific rules; the next five – note-taking only in the target language. After the task is completed, students discuss the main problems encountered. A few classes later the exercise may be repeated with the use of a text in a foreign language.

Exercise 5: Dictation

Aims: developing split attention, practising the use of symbols
Students are asked to prepare sets of ten concepts and symbols on separate sheets. In pairs, they exchange the prepared lists. Student 1 starts by explaining to student 2 the associations behind his/her symbols. Then, for about 1–2 minutes, student 2 reads the concepts from student 1's list in any order (which he/she notes down), and student 1 tries to write them down using symbols. At the end, they both try to check the accuracy of their notes. After achieving 100% accuracy, student 2 repeats the process, changing the order and reducing the time intervals between reading the concepts. Then students swap roles.

Exercise 6: Masters of charades

Aims: practising the use of symbols, memory training, optimizing the layout of notes
In a brainstorming session, students make a list of 20–30 concepts (depending on the level of the group, the concepts may be limited to one specific field), for which they then create symbols. Only five of the proposed concepts can be left without symbols. Then everyone is asked to form longer sentences containing as many of the selected concepts as possible, and to write them down. One by one, each student writes down their sentences on the board, using symbols, and the group has to guess their meaning.

Exercise 7: It's an order!

Aims: developing split attention, practising condensation skills and the use of symbols, optimizing the layout of notes
Students prepare several-minute speeches on a given topic, they work in pairs and deliver the speech to their partner (in 1–2 minute chunks), while the partner is taking notes. Before the presentation, they agree on a set of signs/commands with which the note-taking student will be able to control the partner's speech. These can be, for example, "slow down", "stop", "repeat the last sentence", "explain". In the latter case, the task of the presenting student is to paraphrase the last sentence to make it easier to understand. When student 1 has finished speaking, student 2 interprets the speech with the aid of the notes taken, and then they swap roles.

7.1.3 Processing in Consecutive Interpreting[77]

Exercise 1: Notes

Aims: memory training, developing the ability to analyze the structure of the text, practising condensation skills, improving selectiveness in note-taking
Students listen to a few minutes of a text of an argumentative nature (e. g. "The advantages and disadvantages of having a cat"). They write down only a few words and then they reconstruct the message from memory. The text should contain as many different information pieces as many concepts students are allowed to note down. Thus students are encouraged to deverbalize and condense the text.

Exercise 2: Summarizing

Aims: developing the ability to analyze the structure of the text, practising condensation skills, improving selectiveness in note-taking
Students are provided with a longer text having a simple and logical structure (with clear markers indicating individual parts, for instance "By way of introduction…", "I will present x arguments…", "In conclusion…", etc.), as well as repeated information. Students listen to the text and then translate it in no more than half the time of the original speech. Note-taking may be allowed depending on the student's level. This exercise is aimed at improving analytical thinking

77 On the basis of: Jelec, Anna. "Rozdział 8: Przetwarzanie w tłumaczeniu konsekutywnym". In: Chmiel, Agnieszka and Przemysław Janikowski (eds.). 2015. *Dydaktyka tłumaczenia ustnego*. Katowice: Stowarzyszenie Inicjatyw Wydawniczych, pp. 167–184.

because students will have to refer to the notes they have made and correct them on the go in order to avoid multiple repetitions and to shorten the speaking time.

Exercise 3: Chain of omissions

Aim: developing condensation skills
The teacher presents a short message or a press release. The task of the first student is to summarize it in such a way so as not to exceed half the length of the original. The next student has to present a shortened version of the previous student, halved again, and so on. The exercise continues until the last person in the group summarizes the original text in just one word. The degree of difficulty of the exercise can be increased by asking students, in addition to shortening, to translate the previous speaker's statement. Students should also be reminded that this exercise is to develop condensation skills, and that a very condensed summary of what is said in the target language is not necessarily a good translation.

Exercise 4: Memory

Aims: memory training, developing stress management skills
A set of cards (that can be arranged in pairs, for example, the same word written in two languages) and a timer should be prepared for each participant in this exercise. Students may prepare such cards themselves. After arranging the shuffled cards face down into any regular geometric figure, the timer is set to a certain number of minutes. The student is to match all cards in pairs in the allotted time, but he/she can only uncover two cards at a time. If these two are not a pair, they are placed face down again. Cards matched correctly in pairs remain face up. The exercise ends when all cards are uncovered or when the allotted time finishes. The difficulty level can be adjusted by increasing the number of cards or reducing the amount of time available.

Exercise 5: Word bingo

Aims: memory training, developing split attention
Students listen to a presentation in their mother tongue. The presentation contains a key word that appears many times in the text. The students' task is to listen, take notes and then translate the speech (divided, for example, into two fragments) and at the same time count how many times the key word appears in the text. The winner is the person who provides the correct number of occurrences of the key word.

Exercise 6: Interrogation

Aims: developing split attention and condensation skills, improving selectiveness in note-taking

Students form groups of three, taking the roles of the speaker, the listener and the interrogator. The speaker improvises a short speech during which the interrogator can take notes. The interrogator then uses the notes to ask the listener questions testing his/her understanding of the text. At the end of the exercise, students may discuss the accuracy of their answers and the difficulty of the text. This exercise, depending on the students' level, can be carried out in one or two languages, for example: the source speech may be in one language, and questions and answers in another.

Exercise 7: Register change

Aims: building lexical resources, developing linguistic flexibility

The teacher prepares some texts of a general nature in the students' mother tongue (this may also be assigned to students as part of their homework). The prepared texts are presented in class in the form of speeches. The students' task is to translate them, preserving the content, but changing the register to either completely informal or completely formal. Students can be encouraged to record their speeches and listen to them later for the evaluation of the register used.

Exercise 8: Reversing the argument

Aims: developing language flexibility, memory training, developing stress management skills

The exercise can be done in pairs or groups. The person designated as the speaker presents three statements, another student is to listen to the statements and negate them (e. g. the speaker: "the cat has a tail and four legs and eats beans"; the translator: "the cat does not have four legs and a tail and does not eat beans"). The degree of difficulty of the exercise can be modified in several ways: by changing the length of the statements (the number of arguments used, grammatical complexity of the sentences), changing the register and adding translation to the task. The use of complex sentences with logical cause and effect relationships will also significantly increase the difficulty of this exercise.

Exercise 10: Dual-tasking

Aims: developing split attention, building lexical resources
Students listen to a speech in a foreign language and at the same time they perform a simple distraction task (e. g. watching a cartoon with or without sound, drawing simple shapes, counting aloud, etc.). After listening, they answer questions to check their understanding of the original speech.

7.1.4 Production in Consecutive Interpreting[78]

Exercise 1: Time is money

Aims: developing condensation skills, practising selectivity in note-taking
The teacher informs the students that the aim of the exercise will be to practise condensation of the speech, and their task will be to reconstruct the speech in the same language. The teacher puts students in pairs and delivers a five-minute speech full of redundant expressions (repetitions, expressions which do not bring any new information, lengthy syntactic structures). All students take notes and start working in pairs. Their task is to reconstruct the speech so that the target version does not last longer than three minutes. While the first person in the pair gives a speech, the second person measures the time and checks whether any important elements have been omitted in the reconstruction. Then they swap roles. Afterwards, students compare the length of their reconstructions and the content elements they decided to shorten or omit altogether.

Exercise 2: Out of context

Aims: developing the ability to maintain coherence
Students work in pairs, each person receives a card with three sentences. The first one is the opening sentence of the speech, the second one is a part of the speech's main body, and the third one is the closing sentence. The task of the first person in the pair is to deliver a two-minute speech that would incorporate each of these sentences. The teacher encourages the speakers to pay special attention to the logical structure of the speech and to use conjunctions and linking phrases (e. g. "so", "for example", "moreover", "on the other hand", etc.). The second person's task is to take notes and then interpret the speech consecutively. Student 1 checks

---

78 On the basis of: Korpal, Paweł. "Rozdział 9: Produkcja w tłumaczeniu konsekutywnym". In: Chmiel, Agnieszka and Przemysław Janikowski (eds.). 2015. *Dydaktyka tłumaczenia ustnego.* Katowice: Stowarzyszenie Inicjatyw Wydawniczych, pp. 185–203.

if all information has been included by the translator in the target language. Then students swap roles. Afterwards, the teacher encourages students to discuss the role of coherence in consecutive interpreting.

Exercise 3: Convince me!

Aims: developing the ability to plan speeches, to analyze the structure of the text, to maintain coherence
The teacher divides the students into two groups. The students' task is to prepare a five-minute speech in their mother tongue on a specific topic, following the structure: the introduction (containing a direct address to listeners), the main body (containing three arguments supporting a given thesis) and the conclusion.

Sample topics:
- it is more profitable to run your own business than to work in a company;
- present arguments for legalization of the death penalty;
- it is better to live on the outskirts of the city than in the centre.

After receiving the topic, one group prepares a speech on it, while the second group prepares the speech defending the opposite thesis (e.g. Group 1: present arguments for the legalization of the death penalty; Group 2: present arguments against the legalization of the death penalty). Then both groups indicate persons who would deliver the speeches in front of the class, while members of the opposing group take notes, and then one person translates the speech consecutively into language B. Then the representative of Group 2 gives his/her speech and the members of Group 1 take notes and then translate the speech into language B.

Exercise 4: Improvisation with taboo elements

Aims: developing linguistic flexibility, practising public speaking
The teacher informs the students they will have to speak on a given topic for one minute. At the beginning of the exercise, the teacher divides the students into pairs. Each student selects the beginning of the sentence from which he/she must begin his/her speech. The student has to speak uninterrupted for one minute, and after that time, which is measured by the partner, he/she has a few seconds to finish the speech in a coherent manner.

Sample beginnings:
"I opened the window and, to my amazement, I saw…"
"It was one in the morning, I got a call and it turned out that…"

"Every time I hang out with my friends from high school…"
"If I won a million zlotys…"

In addition to the beginning of the sentence, each card that students draw contains two words that the student must not use during the speech. The words are semantically related to the content of the sentence. For example, in the speech starting with the sentence "If I won a million zlotys…", it is forbidden to use the words "buy" and "money". The task of the other person in the pair is to listen carefully to what the partner is saying and to monitor if the forbidden words are not used. Then the roles are swapped and student 2 draws the card and delivers his/her speech, and student 1 monitors his/her work and offers feedback after the speech is completed.

Exercise 5: Borrowed notes

Aims: practising using symbols, maintaining consistency, optimizing the layout of notes
Students work in pairs. In two or three sentences, the teacher introduces the students to the topic of the speech that he/she is about to give. After this introduction, he/she asks one person from each pair to leave the room. He/she then proceeds to deliver an approximately four-minute speech in language B, for which students are taking notes. After the speech, students who left the room come back and join their partners. Their task is to try to reconstruct the speech (in the same language) based on their partners' notes. Before speaking, they have one minute to read their partner's notes and then start reconstructing the text. The time to read the notes is measured by the teacher using the timer. When each speaker has finished their speech, the students discuss with the teacher the fidelity of the reconstruction. In the second part of the exercise the roles in pairs are swapped.

Exercise 6: Word list

Aims: developing language flexibility, developing planning and public speaking skills, maintaining consistency
Students select five nouns from the set previously prepared by the teacher and deliver a coherent speech in which each of these nouns is used. The order in which the given words appear in the speech is up to the student. The student has about three minutes to familiarize him/herself with the words and come up with the speech, after which, facing the other students and remembering about eye contact and proper posture, he/she delivers the speech. Other students take notes and then translate the text consecutively.

Exercise 7: Not so fast!

Aims: developing stress management skills and public speaking skills
The main purpose of the exercise is to familiarize students with potentially stressful interpreting conditions. The task is to perform consecutive interpreting in a standing position. The student-interpreter is facing the other students and has a notebook to use. The speech given by the teacher is easy at the beginning and does not contain any difficult terms. However, the fragments spoken in the second part are uttered much faster.

7.2 Simultaneous Interpreting

7.2.1 Parainterpreting Exercises[79]

Exercise 1: Shadowing

Aims: developing split attention, memory training
Students repeat the text in the original language with a few-second delay to allow them to understand the text. In the native language this is quite an easy exercise (except for very fast texts), in a foreign language it is more difficult. It is also used to practise listening comprehension, intonation, as well as correct pronunciation of individual words.

Exercise 2: Shadowing with gap filling

Aims: memory training, practising split attention and predictive skills
The teacher removes some words from the source text (ones that are possible to be reconstructed on the basis of the context) and during shadowing students have to complete the gaps (gaps might be indicated with a sound signal).

Sample text in Polish:
Cmentarzysko odkryte w lipcu 2013 roku w Gliwicach może być największym skupiskiem grobów wampirów w Europie. Ale już wcześniej znajdowano u nas XXXXXX (szkielety/ciała/zwłoki) z drewnianymi kołkami w miejscu serca, ze skrępowanymi nogami i odciętymi głowami.

---

79 On the basis of: Bartłomiejczyk, Magdalena. "Rozdział 10: Wprowadzenie tłumaczenia symultanicznego". In: Chmiel, Agnieszka and Przemysław Janikowski (eds.). 2015. *Dydaktyka tłumaczenia ustnego*. Katowice: Stowarzyszenie Inicjatyw Wydawniczych, pp. 207–220.

To miały być typowe wykopaliska ratunkowe, których przeprowadza się w Polsce dziesiątki, np. przy budowie dróg. Jednak stały się XXXXXX (znane/sławne) na całym świecie. XXXXXX (archeolodzy/ naukowcy) natrafili na niezwykły grób człowieka z odciętą głową, czaszka leżała pomiędzy kośćmi nóg szkieletu. Potem zaczęli odkrywać kolejne XXXXXX (groby/ciała/zwłoki/szkielety) ludzi z odciętymi głowami, a wśród nich kobiety z nadpalonymi kośćmi.

Wtedy stało się jasne, że to może być XXXX (cmentarz/cmentarzysko) osób uznanych przed setkami lat za wampiry.

Do dziś w Gliwicach XXXXXX (znaleziono/odkryto/odkopano) szczątki 14 osób. Przy nadpalonych zwłokach kobiety była sprzączka i paciorek, które pozwolą określić wiek znaleziska.

Archeolodzy znajdują groby wampirów u nas i w innych XXXXXX (krajach/ państwach) słowiańskich. Stąd najprawdopodobniej lęk przed wampirami rozprzestrzenił się na całą Europę.

Kiedy powstała wiara w upiorne postaci wysysające XXXXXX (krew) z ludzi? Z całą pewnością jeszcze zanim na polskich ziemiach rozpowszechniło się chrześcijaństwo, postać XXXXXX (wampira) była obecna w przekazywanych z pokolenia na pokolenie podaniach i opowieściach. Wyobrażano go sobie jako żywego trupa, który wstawał z XXXXXX (grobu/trumny) i nawiedzał siedziby ludzi, aby napastować śpiących i wysysać z nich krew.

Exercise 3: Paraphrasing

Aims: memory training, developing split attention and linguistic flexibility
Students paraphrase the content of the source text in the same language, in the form maximally different from the original. This entails the use of synonyms, grammatical transformations (e.g. active instead of passive voice, verb instead of noun structures), changing the order of the elements, etc. Alternatively, the speech register may be changed, for example from formal to colloquial.

Exercise 4: A question and answer session

Aim: developing split attention
The teacher records a series of (20–40) easy questions in a foreign language, for example: "Is the day longer in winter than in summer?". These questions are separated by pauses of about three seconds (or shorter if the teacher wants to increase the difficulty level). The students' task is to answer all questions in full sentences (for example: "No, the day isn't longer/ is shorter in winter than in summer"). In this way, the answers and questions partially overlap, and by answering one question, the student is forced to listen to the next one. The next step is to answer a series of questions about causes of certain phenomena (e.g.:

"Why do we have to feed our pets?"). Students start their answer with "because" and provide the first reason that comes to their mind (e.g.: "Because without food they would die").

Exercise 5: One in mind, two in mind

Aims: developing memory, building lexical resources
The teacher records a series of unrelated words in a foreign language separated by about a second (e.g. table, cat, book...). The students' task is to translate the words they hear, but always with a one-word delay (e.g. after the word "table" they say nothing, after the word "cat" they say "stół", after the word "book" they say "kot", etc.). The next step is to translate a similar series of words in the same way, but this time from their mother tongue into the foreign language. In order to increase the difficulty level, the teacher may ask the students to translate the words with a two-word delay (meaning that, based on the example above, they say nothing after the word "table" or "cat" and only after the word "book" are they supposed to say "stół").

Exercise 6: Listen and count

Aims: developing split attention
Option 1: Students listen to the text aimed at testing listening comprehension, and at the same time they count down aloud starting from any chosen three-digit number. Then they answer comprehension questions (e.g. in the form of a multiple-choice test).

Option 2: Students count down aloud starting from a selected three-digit number while listening to one designated student talking about some event (for example, a recent trip they took). Then they leave the booths and summarize what they remember from the text.

The exercise is more difficult if it is done in two languages, i.e. students count in their native language and listen to a text in a foreign language or vice versa.

7.2.2   Processing in Simultanoues Interpreting[80]

Exercise 1: Medium

Aim: developing anticipation skills
Before listening to any text intended for practising simultaneous interpreting, students may spend a few minutes anticipating its content. The teacher may present the topic of the speech and ask students what kind of content they expect to hear. The discussion may take the form of a brainstorming session with individual ideas being written on the board. After listening to the text and interpreting it, students verify the extent to which the previously anticipated content appeared in the speech.

Exercise 2: Public figure

Aims: developing anticipation skills, broadening the general knowledge
Students prepare at home (or improvise in class) five-minute speeches delivered by famous people on current topics. The student-speaker introduces him/herself and the topic of the speech. Other students predict the content of the speech based on what they know about the given person. They write their ideas down. This is followed by the traditional simultaneous interpreting exercise. Afterwards, the students comment on the results of their predictions.

Exercise 3: Once upon a word

Aims: developing anticipation skills, building lexical resources
The student-speaker presents the topic of his/her speech and its short context. Other students have two minutes to create a possibly longest list of words that may appear in this speech. The words are written in the source language of the speech. Then the list of words can be used to activate the vocabulary. The first student says a word from the list, and the next student introduces its equivalent in the target language (equivalents should be selected according to the context) and then reads a word from his/her list for the next student, etc. The exercise lasts until all the words in the lists have been exhausted. After interpreting the speech, students mark on their lists those words that they predicted correctly.

---

80 On the basis of: Chmiel, Agnieszka. "Rozdział 11: Przetwarzanie w tłumaczeniu symultanicznym". In: Chmiel, Agnieszka and Przemysław Janikowski (eds.). 2015. *Dydaktyka tłumaczenia ustnego*. Katowice: Stowarzyszenie Inicjatyw Wydawniczych, pp. 227–247.

Exercise 4: Gap filling

Aims: developing anticipation skills, practising linguistic flexibility
Students prepare lists of ten collocations (in their native language or the foreign one). It should be made clear beforehand that these need to be phraseological units whose elements are closely tied together and whose meaning results from the sum of the meanings of the individual words, and is not – as is the case of idioms – independent of word meanings. Collocations used in this exercise should be phrases containing a verb. In addition to these lists, students also prepare short texts featuring these collocations. They present them to other students in a written form but with verbs removed. The task is to read the sentences and at the same time complete the gaps with the missing verbs. Such texts can then be used for simultaneous interpretation.

Exercise 5: A postman

Aim: improving delay adjustment
The teacher reads a ten-minute text in a foreign language, which contains enumerations. For this purpose he/she may use, for instance, materials related to exhibition events or present a list of countries participating in a given trade fair. Students interpret the text simultaneously, remembering to shorten the interpretation while rendering the enumerations, and formulate the sentence introducing the enumeration so that its elements can be provided in the nominative form.

Exercise 6: Layers

Aims: improving delay adjustment, developing language flexibility
Students prepare short speeches in Polish, full of sentences having complex syntax and word order different from the typical English: subject – verb – object. During simultaneous interpretation students try to maintain the delay that would be as long as possible compared to the source text.

Exercise 7: Nomen omen

Aims: developing the ability to process proper names, practising public speaking and delay adjustment
The student-speaker delivers a ten-minute speech for the opening of the conference, on the basis of the full programme received from the teacher. The programme features information about the title of the conference, sponsors, guests of honour, timetable and titles of individual speeches, names and titles of

the speakers, as well as the names of the institutions they represent. All this information is included in the speech. However, the speaker should be made aware not to read the programme from a piece of paper. Students interpret the speech simultaneously without any preparation (a more difficult version) or with the text of an incomplete programme in front of them (an easier version). Students can also be asked to prepare these conference programmes with some humorous elements (such as coming up with amusing names of conference guests).

Exercise 8: Numbers

Aims: developing number processing skills, teamwork, improving delay adjustment
The teacher reads a ten-minute text (in the mother tongue or a foreign language) containing a lot of numerical and statistical data. The text may be prepared, for instance, on the basis of statistical yearbooks (birth rate in different countries, fertility rate, life expectancy, GDP generated by different sectors of the economy, etc.), or encyclopaedic data about a given country (population number, population density, historical data, populations of the largest cities, the longest river, the highest peak, etc.). It is important to provide all numbers as accurately as possible so that students have the opportunity to use generalization techniques and to round the numbers. Students interpret the text in the booths in pairs, with the currently non-interpreting student assisting his/her partner by writing down the numbers. Afterwards, when discussing their interpretation experience, students describe their collaboration with the partner, as well as the techniques applied, by answering the following questions: Did your rely on the numbers your partner was writing? Did you use visualization? Which technique proved to be the most effective?

Exercise 9: Overheard

Aims: developing split attention, processing numbers
For this exercise, the teacher needs to prepare another ten-minute text with numbers. This time the students are working in booths separately, and each of them has an assigned student evaluator. Each evaluating student receives a sheet with a table containing all the numbers that appear in the text. The listener's task is to check whether all the numbers have been interpreted correctly (exactly or with the use of generalization), as well as write down what a given number referred to (only on the basis of the interpretation, not the source text). When discussing the interpretation afterwards, points can be awarded for each well-interpreted number and its context.

Exercise 10: An idiom within an idiom

Aims: building lexical resources, developing public speaking skills
As homework, students prepare a list of ten idioms in Polish. The teacher may assign a specific category to each student, e.g. sports, mythological, biblical, literary idioms, etc. In class, students try to find equivalents to these idioms or suggest paraphrases in a foreign language. Then they exchange the lists and make short speeches, which would contain at least half of the idioms included on the list received. The speeches are then used as texts for simultaneous interpreting. A similar exercise may be done with the languages reversed (i.e. the original lists contain idioms in a foreign language, and the interpretation is performed into Polish). Alternatively, the speeches prepared by students may contain incorrect (and often amusing) idioms. This may serve as an exercise for keeping serious face in the booth, or as an exercise aimed at spotting and correcting errors.

Exercise 11: Glossary

Aims: developing planning skills, practising public speaking, building lexical resources, expanding expertise
Students prepare speeches related to the selected theme (half of the speech in the foreign language, the other half in their mother tongue – this way they will have texts that are partially parallel, that is, concerning the same topic but created as source texts in two different languages). Earlier on, they provide their classmates with glossaries for their speeches. In order to motivate students to learn all terms, the teacher may check their knowledge at the beginning of the class in the form of a mini-test. In the preparation stage students not only familiarize themselves with glossaries, but also organize them in a certain way (e.g. combine them into one alphabetically-arranged list, or arrange the speeches in order of their delivery). The texts are then interpreted in class, students use glossaries while interpreting, and afterwards they discuss their solutions.

Activity 12: The big scam

Aims: developing planning skills, practising public speaking, building lexical resources
The student or teacher prepares the text (in the native or a foreign language), in which there are terms that are difficult to translate (including non-existent words invented only for the purpose of the exercise). The meaning of some of them can be guessed from the context, while others remain a mystery. The students' task is to perform a smooth interpretation by applying the previously discussed techniques for solving vocabulary problems.

Exercise 13: Quotes

Aims: developing planning skills, practising public speaking, identifying allusions

Students prepare five-minute speeches (half of the group prepares a speech in the mother tongue, the other half in a foreign language) containing quotes selected according to the following criteria:

- well-known quotes having a recognized translation;
- quotes from the culture of the source language;
- quotes that in the language of the speech are actually translations from the target language;
- quotes from the Bible;
- other quotes.

The speeches are interpreted simultaneously and afterwards students analyze techniques used and assess their effectiveness.

Exercise 14: Haircut

Aims: developing split attention, practising condensation skills

Students receive a text of the speech and familiarize themselves with it, highlighting the most important elements. Then they perform a sight translation of the text, significantly reducing the content (the teacher may specify that the translation should be shortened by 30% or even by half compared to the original version). During the next class they interpret the text simultaneously without having access to the text.

Exercise 15: Turning up the pace

Aims: developing linguistic flexibility, stress management skills, condensation skills, improving delay adjustment

The teacher prepares four texts having a similar content and structure (e.g. descriptions of selected European capital cities). He/she records them with a different speed: the first text at 90 words per minute, the second one – 110 words per minute, the third one – 130, and the fourth one – 150). In case of difficulties with the delivery of the text at the right pace the teacher may use an audio processing programme. Students interpret the texts in the order from the slowest to the fastest one. Each interpretation is followed by a discussion about the text condensation options used by the students.

Activity 16: Non-standard accents

Aim: developing listening comprehension skills

Students find recordings of statements in a foreign language with different accents. Before interpreting a given recording the whole group tries to predict what kind of pronunciation errors or deviations from the standard may appear there. For instance, a Japanese person speaking English would be expected to mix /l/ and /r/ sounds, and when listening to a Frenchman, one may predict the omission of the /h/ sound. While discussing the interpretation, all these predictions are verified.

7.2.3 Production in Simultaneous Interpreting[81]

Exercise 1: In other words

Aims: developing the ability to analyze the structure of the text, building lexical resources

Students bring a short text to the class (of about 800 characters with spaces) related to the current events. They work in pairs, swapping texts. Students scan their texts in search of key information. At this stage, which lasts of up to two minutes, they underline key words (dates, proper names, etc.). During the next three minutes, the students underline linking words or add them where they are not explicitly stated. Then student 1 faithfully reproduces the prepared text to student 2 in the source language, trying to replace the underlined elements with their synonyms, while preserving the meaning of the source text. Student 2 checks the accuracy of the reformulation in relation to the original. After completing the exercise, student 2 assesses the accuracy and coherence of the partner's statements and together they analyze the most accurate solutions and some alternative ways of paraphrasing the difficult elements. Then the students swap roles. The teacher monitors the students while they work, and then encourages the entire group to make a list of challenges and solutions, in the form of a "brainstorming" session, which are then written down on the board for students to copy.

---

81 On the basis of: Gorszczyńska, Paula. "Rozdział 12: Produkcja w tłumaczeniu symultanicznym". In: Chmiel, Agnieszka and Przemysław Janikowski (eds.). 2015. *Dydaktyka tłumaczenia ustnego*. Katowice: Stowarzyszenie Inicjatyw Wydawniczych, pp. 248–269.

Exercise 2: Re-registration

Aims: developing language flexibility and the ability to analyze the structure of the text

Students write a short text on a previously assigned topic, for example, the social media. Then, having exchanged texts, they work in pairs. The task of student 1 is to present the text of student 2, without preparation, in a register higher than the original one. The teacher may suggest a situation where such a register is typically used (e. g. an academic lecture, a presentation at an academic conference, etc.). Student 2 listens carefully to assess how successfully student 1 completed the task. Then student 2 presents the text of student 1 using a lower register. The teacher again may suggest a situation in which such a register is in use (e. g. an argument between middle school pupils on the school playground, a casual conversation on the tram, etc.). After completing the task, students discuss it in pairs. Then the teacher asks the entire group about the features of the individual registers and writes them down on the board for students to copy.

Exercise 3: Poker face

Aims: building lexical resources, developing linguistic flexibility and stress management skills

Student 1 improvises a short speech in a given register, on a given topic, based on visual materials. At the same time student 2 shows him/her, in about 10-second intervals, sheets of paper with a single word or phrase that the improviser is intended to include to his/her speech without affecting its fluency, and showing no signs of annoyance or amusement. Student 3, not seeing the words shown by student 2, listens to the improvisation and tries to guess which words used in an improvised utterance were those shown by student 2. After improvisation, students verify the predictions of student 3 and evaluate the speech of student 1 in terms of register.

Exercise 4: Short and to the point

Aims: memory training, practising condensation skills, analyzing text structure

In preparation for simultaneous interpreting of speeches delivered at a fast pace, the teacher asks students to brainstorm the ways of coping with this type of situation. He/she may elicit such techniques as: intentionally delaying the start of the interpretation in order to gain a broader perspective of the source text; omitting the irrelevant repetitions and rhetorical devices considered unnecessary for conveying the overall meaning; shortening the names of organizations, institutions, programmes or documents to acronyms or key nouns (e. g. using just the word "office" if a given fragment of the source text refers to a single institution of this type); shortening the lists of elements illustrating the issue in question to, for instance, only three; using pronouns and other abbreviated references to refer to the previously described phenomena, etc. Then, students, working in pairs or groups of three where one person plays the role of the interpreter and the others take the role of listeners, interpret in a whispered mode the speech delivered by the teacher at a fast pace. As a follow-up of this activity there is an evaluation session.

Exercise 5: Padding the text

Aims: developing linguistic flexibility, developing the ability to monitor the speech, practising explication
The student, while skimming a two-sentence text, reads it, filling it with words that are "semantically empty". In addition to such "padding", the student is also allowed to use explication, for example in the form of descriptive expressions and other multi-word structures replacing single words, and to clarify information that is potentially unclear to the recipient. When student 1 finishes a given sentence, student 2, playing a role of a curious child, may ask questions stimulating further development of the text. His/her role is also to note any occurrence of a vocalized pause or a nervous grunt. The exercise finishes with an evaluation session.

Activity 6: Taboo

Aims: memory training, developing linguistic flexibility, practising anticipation skills
The teacher prepares short texts to which he/she assigns numbers. On a piece of paper with the number of a given text, he/she writes a list of 10 forbidden words in the target language. Students have 30 seconds to read the list. Then the teacher takes the list from one of the students, and him/herself reads the text in the source language. The task of the student without the list is to interpret the text into the target language, without using any of the forbidden words. If he/she does, other students need to interrupt and help him/her find a synonym. Meanwhile, students listening to the interpretation may list synonyms or other solutions. The teacher evaluates the interpretation and discusses with students the ideas for replacing the forbidden words.

Exercise 7: Tomato

Aims: developing linguistic flexibility, practising anticipation skills

As their homework, students prepare texts with gaps that others should be able to guess on the basis of the context or their general knowledge. In class, the student reads the prepared text, filling in the gaps with a previously agreed sound signal or words unrelated to the topic of the text (e. g. "pomidor" in the Polish version or "banana" in the English version). Other students, depending on the level, paraphrase or interpret the text simultaneously, replacing the sound or word signals with the correct equivalents. Then they listen to the recordings and compare their interpretation with the original displayed on the board or distributed to them as a printout. The teacher encourages students to discuss what motivated their individual lexical choices.

Exercise 8: Machinations

Aims: developing linguistic flexibility, improving delay regulation

The teacher discusses examples of acceptable manipulations of the word order in the target (foreign) language, illustrating on the board the possible positions of a given structure within a sentence.

Example:
a) Panellists, as provided in the conference programme, will now respond to delegate questions.
b) As provided in the conference programme, panellists will now respond to delegates' questions.
c) Panellists will now answer delegates' questions, as provided in the conference programme.

The teacher then encourages students to think about similar structures in their mother tongue. Together, they create a list of elements that undergo the procedure of word order change without affecting the meaning of the sentence. Students interpret *a vista* the texts prepared by the teacher, containing phrases or expressions belonging to the categories discussed. Then they create their own speeches to deliver as source texts for other students to interpret. The interpreters' task is to position a phrase of a given type in the target text in a different place within the sentence than in the original. Each attempt is followed with a discussion of difficulties encountered and effective solutions.

Exercise 9: Mind control

Aims: developing linguistic flexibility, practising anticipation skills

The teacher prepares a recorded text in which the selected units of meaning could be interpreted in a way that breaks the structure of the source text (in English these could be e. g. dates, subjects requiring the use of the active voice, etc.). The task of the students performing simultaneous interpretation is to obey the word order imposed by the beginnings of sentences, as displayed by the teacher on paper, or using the projector. Then the students listen to their own or their cabin partner's recorded interpretation, paying special attention to and assessing its syntactic accuracy.

Example:

Source text:
(1) It is incredible how many people visit gossip Internet sites.
(2) The number of Polish Internet users who in 2010 declared at least one visit per day to this type of site seems unreal.
(3) Viewed by many millions are primarily sites that describe lives of celebrities.

Sample hints:
(1) Sites... or: Number...
(2) In 2010... or: Internet users
(3) Many millions...

Exercise 10: Mind reading

Aims: developing linguistic flexibility, practising anticipation skills

The teacher prepares a series of sentences related with each other. Students work in pairs. The teacher, having informed the students beforehand about the topic and the structure of the text, provides student 1 with the beginning of the first sentence, asking him/her to repeat it and finish it. At the same time, student 2 interprets this sentence simultaneously and records the interpretation. Then the teacher reads the beginning of the second sentence, giving students time to repeat it and complete it in a way that would be a logical continuation of the message expressed in the previous sentence. Student 2 continues the interpretation, paying attention to fluency and coherence. These steps are repeated until the last sentence. Then students in pairs listen to the interpretations. Afterwards, the teacher reads the original version. Finally, the teacher discusses with the students the alternatives applied by students 1 in the source language and those suggested by students 2 in the target language. All these solutions are evaluated in terms of the logic, grammatical accuracy, as well as register.

Example:
W szalonym pędzie codzienności wiedziemy... (np. żywot niewolników czasu). Balansując na... (np. krawędzi wyczerpania), nie zważamy... (np. na zagrożenia związane z ciągłym narażeniem na stres). Tymczasem stresowi... (np. przypisuje się winę...), itd.

Exercise 11: Segmentation

Aims: developing linguistic flexibility, improving delay regulation
The teacher asks the students to simultaneously interpret a speech read at a fast pace, having the syntax of a written language (long, complex sentences, unnatural for speech). Seeing their resignation after a failed attempt to do the impossible, i. e. to interpret 100% of the content and form, the teacher explains the segmentation technique to the students. In the next stage of this exercise, students listen to the individual sentences of the text in isolation, and at a slightly slower pace. Their task is to create the shortest sentences possible as soon as they hear a unit of meaning. The teacher gradually speeds up the pace of reading. Then the students work on the printed text of the speech, dividing it into shorter sentences and giving them the character of a spoken text (changing the order of subordinate clauses, adding connectors, etc.). The text prepared in this way is then interpreted *a vista* by the students.

Exercise 12: Collocation fight

Aims: developing linguistic flexibility, practising anticipation skills
Students, using their mother tongue, write down on small cards certain collocations related to a thematic scope or a specific word given by the teacher (e. g. the word "idea": *to come up with an idea, to put forward an idea, to reject an idea, to challenge an idea, to accept an idea, to implement an idea, to multiply ideas, an/a interesting/good/genius/great idea, a bad/bad/ridiculous/stupid idea*, etc.), then they put the cards face down. On the second pile, the teacher places cards depicting people, professions, places, etc. (the so-called "hints"). Students are divided into two teams (A and B), and they "play" in turns according to the following rules: the first person from team A draws one collocation and one hint card and, on the basis of them, he/she formulates a sentence which will be the beginning of the story or just an independent sentence, according to the format agreed before the start of the game. Then the first person on the team B interprets this sentence. At the same time, a committee of two students verifies the accuracy

of the interpretation and awards a point for each correct one. When in doubt, the committee members show a yellow card to ask the other players for help in making a decision, and in the case of a clearly incorrect interpretation, they show a red card, which means no point for the interpreter's team. The next student to draw the cards is the previous interpreter's neighbour, that is, another person from team B. The teacher monitors the dynamics of the game and he/she prepares a glossary to be completed after the game is finished.

References

Ackermann, Dorothea. 1998. "On the Assessment of Students' Interpreting Performance and Its Role in Interpreting Training". In: *Ocena tłumaczenia ustnego/Evaluating an Interpreter's Performance*, edited by James Hartzell, 157–166. Łódź: Centre for Modern Translation and Interpretation Studies, 1998.

Agrifoglio, Marjorie. "Sight Translation and Interpreting. A Comparative Analysis of Constraints and Failures". In *Interpreting* 6, no. 1 (2004): 43–67.

Ashouri, Marzieh, Bahri, Hossein, and Esmat Babaii. "The Relationship Between Selective Attention and Simultaneous Interpreting Performance in Undergraduate Students of Translation". In *Iranian Journal of Applied Linguistics (IJAL)* 24, no. 1 (2021): 67–102.

Atkinson, Richard L., and Richard M. Shiffrin. "Human Memory: A Proposed System and Its Control Processes". In *The psychology of learning and motivation,* vol. 2, edited by Kenneth W. Spence and Janet Taylor Spence. London: Academic Press, 1968.

Baigorri-Jalón, Jesús. "Perspectives on the History of Interpretation: Research Proposals". In *Charting the Future of Translation History,* edited by Georges L. Bastin, and Paul F. Bandia, 101–110. University of Ottawa Press, 2006.

Ballester, Ana, and Cartalina Jimenez Hurtado. "Approaches to the Teaching of Interpreting". In *Teaching Translation and Interpreting: Training Talent and Experience.* Papers from the First Language International Conference, Elsinore, Denmark, 1992.

Barik, Henri C. "Simultaneous Interpretation: Qualitative and Linguistic Data". In *The Interpreting Studies Reader,* edited by Franz Pöchhacker and Miriam Shlesinger, 79–91. London/New York: Routledge, 1975/2002.

Barron, Frank. "Putting Creativity to Work". In *The Nature of Creativity. Contemporary Psychological Perspectives*, edited by Robert J. Sternberg, 76–98. Cambridge: Cambridge University Press, 1988.

Camayd-Freixas, Erik. "Cognitive Theory of Simultaneous Interpreting and Training". Proceedings of the 52nd Conference of the American Translators Association. New York: ATA, 2011.

Cartellieri, Claus. "The Inescapable Dilemma: Quality and/or Quantity in Interpreting". In *Babel* 29, no. 4.(1983): 209–213.

Čeňková, Ivana. 2010. "Sight Translation" In *Handbook of Translation Studies,* Vol 1, edited by Yves Gambier and Luc van Doorslaer, 320–323. Amsterdam/Philadelphia: John Benjamins Publishing Company, 2010.

Chernov, Ghelly V. *Inference and Anticipation in Simultaneous Interpreting.* Amsterdam/ Philadelphia: John Benjamins Publishing Company, 2004.

Chernov, Ghelly V. "Message Redundancy and Message Anticipation in Simultaneous Interpretation". In *Bridging the Gap*, edited by Sylvie Lambert and Barbara Moser-Mercer, 139–153. Amsterdam/ Philadelphia: John Benjamins Publishing Company, 1994.

Chmiel, Agnieszka, and Przemysław Janikowski (eds.). *Dydaktyka tłumaczenia ustnego.* Katowice: Stowarzyszenie Inicjatyw Wydawniczych, 2015.

Cho, Sang-Eun. "Translator's Creativity Found in the Process of Japanese-Korean Translation". In *Meta: Translators' Journal* 51, no. 2 (2006): 378–388.

Collados Aís, Ángela. "Quality Assessment in Simultaneous Interpreting: The Importance of Nonverbal Communication". In: *The Interpreting Studies Reader*, edited by Franz Pöchhacker and Miriam Shlesinger, 327–336. London/New York: Routledge, 1998/2002.

Cox, David. *Kreatywne myślenie dla bystrzyków.* Gliwice: Helion, 2015.

Darò, Valeria, and Franco Fabbro. "Verbal Memory During Simultaneous Interpretation: Effects of Phonological Interference". In *Applied Linguistics* 15, no. 4 (1994): 365–381.

Darò, Valeria, Lambert, Sylvie, and Franco Fabbro. "Conscious Monitoring of Attention during Simultaneous Interpreting". In *Interpreting* 1, no. 1 (1996): 101–124.

Déjean Le Féal, Karla. "L'enseignement des méthodes d'interprétation". In *L'enseignement de l'interprétation et de la traduction: de la théorie à la pédagogie*, edited by Jean Delisle, 23–46. Ottawa: Éditions de l'Université de Ottawa, 1981.

Déjean Le Féal, Karla. "La liberté en interprétation". In *La liberté en transduction*, edited by Fortunato Israël and Marianne Lederer, 211–219. Paris: Didier Erudition, 1991.

Dragsted, Barbara, and Inge Gorm Hansen. "Exploring Translation and Interpreting Hybrids. The Case of Sight Translation". In *Meta: Translators' Journal* 54, no. 3 (2009): 588–604.

Dublanc, Davide. "Tłumaczenie ustne: początki i rozwój". In *Iuvenilia Philologorum Cracoviensium*, vol. 1, *Źródła Humanistyki Europejskiej*, Kraków: Wydawnictwo Uniwersytetu Jagiellońskiego, 2008.

Eunson, Baden. *Communicating in the 21st Century.* (2nd ed.). Australia: John Wiley & Sons, 2008.

Eysenck, Hans Jürgen. *Genius: the Natural History of Creativity.* Cambridge: Cambridge University Press, 1995.

Ferryanti, Ni Putu. "The Analysis of Transferring Message in Consecutive Interpreting on Bilingual Seminar Held by SMK Dwijendra Denpasar Bali". In *Widya Accarya* 8, no. 2, 2017.

Gabora, Liane. "Cognitive Mechanisms Underlying the Creative Process". In *Proceeding of the Fourth Conference on Creativity and Cognition*, edited by Thomas T. Hewett, and Terence Kavanagh, 126–133. Loughborough University, UK, 2002.

Gile, Daniel. "Simultaneous Interpreting". In *An Encyclopedia of Practical Translation and Interpreting*, edited by Sin-wai Chan, 531–561. Hong Kong: The Chinese University Press, 2018.

Gile, Daniel. "Teaching Conference Interpreting: A Contribution". In *Training for the New Millennium: Pedagogies for Translation and Interpreting*, edited by Martha Tennent, 127–151. Amsterdam/Philadelphia: John Benjamin Publishing Company, 2005.

Gile, Daniel. *Basic Concepts and Models for Interpreter and Translator Training*. Amsterdam/Philadelphia: John Benjamins Publishing Company, 2009.

Gillies, Andrew. *Conference Interpreting*, edited by Bartosz Waliczek, Kraków: Tertium, 2004.

Gillies, Andrew. *Note-Taking for Consecutive Interpreting – A Short Course*. Manchester: St. Jerome Publishing, 2005.

Gruber, Hoard E., and Sara N. Davis. "Inching Our Way Up Mount Olympus: the Evolving-Systems Approach to Creative Thinking". In *The nature of Creativity. Contemporary Psychological Perspectives*, edited by Robert J. Sternberg, 243–270. Cambridge: Cambridge University Press, 1988.

Hale, Sandra. *Community Interpreting*. Springer, 2007.

Harris, Brian. 1990. "Norms in Interpretation". In *Target* 2, no. 1 (1990): 115–119.

Hejwowski, Krzysztof. *Kognitywno-komunikacyjna teoria przekładu*. Warszawa: Wydawnictwo Naukowe PWN, 2004.

Horváth, Ildikó. *Interpreter Behaviour. A Psychological Approach*. Budapest, Hang Nyelviskola Bt., 2012.

Kakas, Gizella B. "Study of the Relationship Between Creativity and Frustration Tolerance". In *Studies in Creativity*, edited by Lajos Kardos, Csaba Pléh and Ilona Barkóczi. Budapest: Akadémiai Kiadó, 1987.

Kalina, Sylvia. "Interpreting Competences as a Basis and a Goal for Teaching". In *The Interpreters' Newsletter* no. 10. EUT – Edizioni Università di Trieste, 2000.

Kiraly, Don. *A Social Constructivist Approach to Translator Education: Empowerment from Theory to Practice*. Manchester/Northampton: St. Jerome Publishing, 2000.

Klimkowska, Katarzyna. *Orientacja na sukces zawodowy studentów kończących studia translatorskie*. Lublin: Wydawnictwo UMCS, 2013.

Komlósi, Annamária. "Creativity and Perception". In *Studies in Creativity*, edited by Lajos Kardos, Csaba Pléh and Ilona Barkóczi, 11–22. Budapest: Akadémiai Kiadó, 1987.

Kopczyński, Andrzej. "Quality in Conference Interpreting". *Translation Studies: An Interdiscipline*, selected papers from the Translation Studies Congress, edited by Mary Snell-Hornby, Franz Pöchhacker and Klaus Kaindl. Vienna, 1994.

Korpal, Paweł. "Stress Experienced by Polish Sworn Translators and Interpreters". In *Perspectives: Studies in Translation Theory and* Practice 29, no. 4 (2021): 554–571.

Korpal, Paweł. 2016. "Interpreting as a Stressful Activity: Physiological Measures of Stress in Simultaneous Interpreting". In *Poznań Studies in Contemporary Linguistics* 52, no. 2 (2016): 297–316.

Kovács, Ágnes. "Creativity of Associations Given to Complex and Simplex Figures in Groups of Different Preference". In *Studies in Creativity*, edited by Lajos Kardos, Csaba Pléh and Ilona Barkóczi, 49–68. Budapest: Akadémiai Kiadó, 1987.

Kraft, Tara L., and Sarah D. Pressman. "Grin and Bear It: the Influence of Manipulated Facial Expression on the Stress Response". In *Psychological Science* 23, no. 11 (2012): 1372–1378.

Kruk-Junger, Katarzyna. "Teaching Norms in Interpreting". In *Między Oryginałem a Przekładem* 22, no. 3(33), (2016): 41–53.

Kurz, Ingrid. "CO2 and O2 Levels in Booths at the End of a Conference Day – A Pilot Study". In *AIIC Bulletin* 11, no. 3 (1983): 86–93.

Kussmaul, Paul. *Training the Translator.* Amsterdam/Philadelphia: John Benjamins Publishing Company, 1995.

Lambert, Sylvie. "Shared Attention during Sight Translation, Sight Interpretation and Simultaneous Interpretation". In *Meta: Translators' Journal* 41, no. 1 (2004): 293–306.

Landau, Erika. *A kreativitás pszichológiája* [The psychology of creativity], Budapest: Tankönyvkiadó, 1976.

Liu, Min-hua. "How do experts interpret? Implications from research in interpreting studies and cognitive science". In *Efforts and Models in Interpreting and Translation Research. A Tribute to Daniel Gile*, edited by Gyde Hanse, Andrew Chesterman, and Heidrun Gerzymisch-Arbogast, 159–177. Amsterdam: John Benjamins Publishing Company, 2008.

Łuczyński, Edward, and Jolanta Maćkiewicz. *Językoznawstwo ogólne.* Gdańsk: Wydawnictwo Uniwersytetu Gdańskiego, 2002.

MacRae, Sheila M. "Information-Crunching and Other Aspects of Interpretation: Technique or Creative Process?". In *Coming of Age.* Proceedings of the 30th Annual Conference of the American Translators Association, edited by Deanna Lindberg Hammond, 149–153. Washington, D. C. Medford, NJ: Learned Information, Inc., 1989.

Mahmoodzadeh Kambiz. "Consecutive Interpreting: Its Principles and Techniques". In: *Teaching Translation and Interpreting*, edited by Cay Dollerup and Annette Loddegaard, 231–236. Amsterdam/Philadelphia: John Benjamins Publishing Company, 1992.

Malau, Putri Pridani; Lubis, Syahron, and Umar Mono. "Errors in Consecutive Interpreting: A Case of Jessica Kumalawongso's Court", In *Language Literacy: Journal of Linguistics, Literature and Language Teaching* 5, no. 1 (2021): 71–79.

Marković, Helena. "Kinesics and Body Language in Simultaneous and Consecutive Interpretation". Master's Thesis. Osijek, 2017.

Maulida, De Lara Siti, and Andang Saehu. "The Procedures of Consecutive Interpreting". In *Linguists: Journal Of Linguistics and Language Teaching* 8, no. 1 (2022): 130–142.

Merlini Raffaela. "Alla ricerca dell'interprete ritrovato". In *Interpretazione di trattativa*, edited by Mariachiara Russo and Gabriele Mack, 19–35. Milano, 2005.

Miletich, Marko. "Accounting for Nonverbal Communication in Interpreter-Mediated Events in Healthcare Settings". In *Translation and Translanguaging in Multilingual Contexts* 1, no. 2 (2015): 162–181.

Nader-Cioszek, Monika. "Tłumaczenie a vista w dydaktyce innych rodzajów translacji". In *Lingwistyka Stosowana* 16, no. 1 (2016): 37–45.

Newmark, Peter. *A Textbook of Translation.* London: Prentice Hall, 1988.

Nolan, James. *Interpretation: Techniques and Exercises.* Multilingual Matters, 2012.

Obidina, Veronika V. "Sight Translation: Typological Insights into the Mode" In *Journal of Siberian Federal University. Humanities & Social Sciences* 1, no. 8 (2015): 91–98.

Pagnoulle, Christine. "Creativity in Non-Literary Translation". In *Perspectives: Studies in Translatology* 1, no. 1 (1993): 79–90.

Peper, Erik; Booiman, Annette; Lin, I-Mei, and Richard Harvey. "Increase Strength and Mood with Posture". In *Biofeedback* 44, no. 2 (2016): 66–72.

Perkins, David N. "The Possibility of Invention". In *The Nature of Creativity. Contemporary Psychological Perspectives*, edited by Robert J. Sternberg, 362–385. Cambridge: Cambridge University Press, 1988.

Peterson, Lloyd R., and Margaret J. Peterson. "Short Term Retention of Individual Items". In *Journal of Experimental Psychology* 58, (1959): 193–198.

Pettersson, Rune. "Attention: An Information Design Perspective". In *Document Design* 2, no. 2 (2001): 114–130.

Phelan, Mary. *The Interpreter's Resource.* Clevedon, Buffalo, Toronto, Sydney: Multilingual Matters Ltd, 2001.

Pöchhacker, Franz. "Getting Organized: The Evolution of Community Interpreting". In *Interpreting* 4, no. 1 (1999): 125–140.

Pöchhacker, Franz. "I in TS: On Partnership in Translation Studies". In *Translation Research and Interpreting Research: Traditions, Gaps and Synergies,* edited by Christina Schäffner, 104–115. Clevedon/Buffalo/Toronto: Multilingual Matters Ltd, 2004.

Pöchhacker, Franz. *Introducing Interpreting Studies* (2nd ed.). Routledge, 2016.

Poyatos, Fernando. *Nonverbal Communication Across Disciplines: Culture, Sensory Interaction, Speech, Conversation,* vol. 1. Amsterdam: John Benjamins Publishing Company, 2002.

Poyatos, Fernando. "The Reality of Multichannel Verbal-Nonverbal Communication in Simultaneous and Consecutive Interpretation". In *Nonverbal Communication and Translation: New Perspectives and Challenges in Literature, Interpretation and the Media,* edited by Fernando Poyatos, 249–282. Amsterdam/Philadelphia: John Benjamins Publishing Company, 1977.

Rennert, Sylvi. "Visual Input in Simultaneous Interpreting". In *Meta: Translators' Journal* 54, no. 1 (2008): 204–217.

Riccardi, Alessandra. "Evaluation in Interpretation: Macrocriteria and Microcriteria". In: Teaching Translation and Interpreting, edited by Eva Hung, 115–126. Amsterdam/Philadelphia: John Benjamins Publishing Company, 2002.

Riccardi, Alessandra. "Interpreting Strategies and Creativity". In *Translators' Strategies and Creativity,* edited by Ann Beylard-Ozeroff, Jana Králová, and Barbara Moser-Mercer, 171–180. Amsterdam/New York: John Benjamins Publishing Company, 1998.

Riccardi, Alessandra. "On the Evolution of Interpreting Strategies in Simultaneous Interpreting", In *Translators' Journal* 50, no 2 (2005): 753–767.

Rozan, Jean-François. *Note-Taking in Consecutive Interpreting,* edited by Andrew Gillies and Bartosz Waliczek. Kraków: Tertium, 2002.

Saehu, Andang. *Interpreting; Teori dan Praktik,* edited by Irwan Kurniawan. Bandung: Nuansa Cendekia Bandung, 2018.

Sandrelli, Annalisa. "New Technologies in Interpreter Training: CAIT". In *Textology and Translation,* edited by Heidrun Gerzymisch-Arbogast et al., 261–289. Tübingen: Gunter Narr Verlag, 2003.

Schank, Roger C. (1988) "Creativity as a Mechanical Process". In *The Nature of Creativity. Contemporary Psychological Perspectives,* edited by Robert J. Sternberg, 220–238. Cambridge: Cambridge University Press, 1988.

Seleskovitch, Danica, and Marianne Lederer. *Pédagogie raisonnée de l'interprétation.* Paris: Didier Erudition, 2002.

Shlesinger, Miriam. "Strategic Allocation of Working Memory and Other Attentional Resources in Simultaneous Interpretation". Unpublished doctoral dissertation, Bar Ilan University, Ramat Gran, Israel, 2000.

Solarczyk-Ambrozik, Ewa. "Znaczenie edukacji uniwersyteckiej dla kształcenia kapitału społecznego studentów". In *Wyzwania współczesnej edukacji dorosłych. Andragogika jako przedmiot akademicki*, edited by Artur Fabiś, 169–174. Mysłowice/Zakopane: Wydawnictwo Górnośląskiej Wyższej Szkoły Pedagogicznej, 2004.

Sternberg, Robert J. *The Nature of Creativity. Contemporary Psychological Perspectives.* Cambridge: Cambridge University Press, 1988.

Szabó, Endre. *Problémamegoldás és kreativitás* [Problem-solving and Creativity], Sopron: Euroqualitas Könyvkiadó, 2002.

Tabakowska, Elżbieta. "Polish Tradition". In *Routledge Encyclopedia of Translation Studies*, edited by Mona Baker, 523–532. London and New York: Routledge, 1998/2001.

Tabakowska, Elżbieta. "Translation Studies and Translator Training in Poland – Past Present and Future". In *Folia Translatologica, International Series of Translation Studies*, vol. 1 (1992): 7–16.

Taylor, Calvin W. "Various Approaches to and Definitions of Creativity". In *The Nature of Creativity. Contemporary Psychological Perspectives*, edited by Robert J. Sternberg, 99–124. Cambridge: Cambridge University Press, 1988.

Tomaszkiewicz, Teresa. *Terminologia tłumaczenia,* edited by Jean Delisle, Hannelore Lee-Jahnke, Jörn Albrecht and Monique C. Cormier. Poznań: Wydawnictwo Naukowe UAM, 2004.

Torrance, Paul E. "The Nature of Creativity as Manifest in Testing". In *The Nature of Creativity. Contemporary Psychological Perspectives,* edited by Robert J. Sternberg, 43–75. Cambridge: Cambridge University Press, 1988.

Tryuk, Małgorzata. "Strategies in Interpreting: Issues, Controversies, Solutions". In: *Lingwistyka Stosowana / Applied Linguistics / Angewandte Linguistik,* vol. 2 (2010): 181–194.

Tryuk, Małgorzata. *Przekład ustny konferencyjny.* Warszawa: PWN, 2007.

Van Hoof, Henry. *Théorie et pratique de l'interprétation.* München: Max Hueber Verlag, 1962.

Viaggio, Sergio. "Kinesics and the Simultaneous Interpreter. The Advantages of Listening with One's Eyes and Speaking with One's Body". In *Nonverbal Communication and Translation: New Perspectives and Challenges in Literature, Interpretation and the Media,* edited by Fernando Poyatos, 283–293. Amsterdam/Philadelphia: John Benjamins Publishing Company, 1997.

Viaggio, Sergio. "The Teacher as Setter of Professional Norms. Some Thoughts on Quality and Quality Assessment in Simultaneous Interpretation". In: *Quality Forum 1997. Esperienze, Problemi, Prospettive,* edited by Maurizio Viezzi, 101–119. Trieste: SSLMIT, 1999.

Viezzi, Maurizio. *Aspetti della Qualità in Interpretazione.* Università degli Studi di. Trieste, Scuola Superiore di Lingue Moderne, 1996.

Walter, Hilmar. "On the Problem of Routine and Creativeness in Translation". In *Translation, our future. La traduction, notre avenir.* Proceedings of the XIth World Congress of FIT, edited by Paul Nekeman, 106–109. Maastricht: Euroterm, 1988.

Weisberg, Robert W. "Problem-Solving and Creativity". In *The Nature of Creativity. Contemporary Psychological Perspectives,* edited by Robert J. Sternberg, 148–176. Cambridge: Cambridge University Press, 1988.

Wickens, Christopher D., and Melody C. Carswell. "Information Processing". In *Handbook of Human Factors and Ergonomics*, Fourth Edition, edited by Gavriel Salvendy, 117–161. John Wiley & Sons: New Jersey, 2012.

Wickens, Christopher D., Juliana Goh, Hohn Helleberg, William J. Horrey, and Donald A. Talleur. "Attentional Models of Multitask Pilot Performance Using Advanced Display Technology". In *Human Factors* 45, no. 3 (2003): 360–380.

Wilss, Wolfram. *Knowledge and Skills in Translational Behaviour*. Amsterdam/Philadelphia: John Benjamins Publishing Company, 1996.

Woodsworth, Judith and Jean Delisle. *Translators through History* (Revised ed.). Amsterdam/Philadelphia: John Benjamins Publishing Company, 2012.

Zabalbeascoa, Patrick. "From Techniques to Types of Solutions". In *Investigating translation,* edited by Allison Beeby, Doris Ensinger, and Marisa Presas, 117–127. Amsterdam/Philadelphia: John Benjamins Publishing Company, 2000.

Zeier, Hans. "Psychophysiological Stress Research". In *Interpreting* 2, no.1/2 (1997): 231–249.

Zhong, Weihe. "Memory Training in Interpreting". In: *Translation Journal* 7, no. 3, 2003.

Zieliński, Lech. "Nauczanie przekładu (tekstów fachowych) na kierunkach neofilologicznych. Stan obecny, perspektywy rozwoju". In *Język trzeciego tysiąclecia* III, vol. 2, *Konteksty przekładowe*, edited by Maria Piotrowska, 429–437. Kraków: Tertium, 2005.

Żmudzki, Jerzy. "Holizm funkcjonalny w perspektywie translatoryki antropocentrycznej". In *Lingwistyka Stosowana/ Applied Linguistics/ Angewandte Linguistik* 8 (2013): 177–188.

Żmudzki, Jerzy. *Blattdolmetschen in paradigmatischer Perspektive der anthropozentrischen Translatorik*. Frankfurt am Main: Peter Lang, 2015.

Online Sources

AIIC Workload Study, 2002. https://aiic.org/document/468/aiicwebzine_febmar2002_7_a iic_interpreter_wo.

Kurz, Ingrid. "Physiological Stress During Simultaneous Interpreting: A Comparison of Experts and Novices". In *The Interpreters' Newsletter* 12, 2003. https://www.researchga te.net/publication/238679007_Physiological_stress_during_simultaneous_interpretin g_A_comparison_of_experts_and_novices.

Practical Guide for Professional Conference Interpreters, 2016. https://aiic.org/documen t/547/AIICWebzine_Apr2004_2_Practical_guide_for_professional_conference_interpr eters_EN.pdf.

Zwischenberger, Cornelia and Franz Pöchhacker. "Survey on Quality and Role: Conference Interpreters' Expectations and Self-Perceptions". In *Communicate!* 53, 2010. https:// aiic.org/document/9646/.